France Without
Reservations

France Without Reservations

An Impromptu Travel Guide

by
Maurice K. Thompson

GATEWAY
BOOKS

Edited and Designed by Donna S. Lee
Cover Design by Amy Neiman
Cover Illustration © by Cynthia Fitting / SIS

Printed in the United States of America

Gateway Books

Distributed by Publishers Group West

Library of Congress Cataloging-in-Publication Data

Thompson, Maurice K.
    France without reservations : an impromptu travel guide / by
Maurice K. Thompson.
        p.   cm.
    Includes index.
    ISBN 0-933469-24-1
    1. France--Guidebooks.   I. Title.
DC16.T46   1995
914.404'839--dc20

95-35906
CIP

10 9 8 7 6 5 4 3 2

To Rae and Howard "Jonah" Jones.
May their enthusiasm for travel and adventure never wane.

Contents

I wish to acknowledge and thank Judith and Don Merwin for their invaluable aid at every step in the preparation of this book, along with particular thanks to Donna Lee for her perceptive editing.

Versailles • • PARIS
• Chartres

Olivet-Orléans •

• Bourges

Aubusson •

• Clermont-Ferrand
• Brioude
• Le Puy

Tulle •
Brive •
Souillac •
Rocamadour •
Villefranche-
de-Rouergue •
Cordes •
Albi • Montpellier
Castres •
Béziers

Alès • Uzès
• • Avignon
• Aix
Vence
Grasse
Marseille • Fréjus
Toulon

Chapter 1

Culture Shock: France

In Paris, one can be rich or one can be poor, but one may never be old. True, the body may twinge from an aching joint, or one's new teeth may not fit as well as could be desired, but these are mechanical things and should not be confused with the spirit to which they are attached. It is this spirit which responds to the French capital with such a heady exhilaration. It is this spirit, somehow too often repressed in Americans, that since the time of Ben Franklin and Thomas Jefferson has found itself liberated by the very thought of Paris. But Paris has more to offer, beyond *joie de vivre*, for it is the gateway to all of France. Even Mark Twain, that classic American cynic, was enchanted by the sheer diversity of this land and people, bound together by little more than a common tongue.

We were again in France, probably for the twentieth time, but as we absorbed the sights, the sounds, and the smells that were both foreign and familiar, the excitement returned, as intense as on our first visit. We drank our morning *café au lait* while standing at a bar, knowing that the price was half that charged those sitting at a table. Avoiding the notorious four-dollar cup of coffee was the kind of *joie de vivre* I appreciated.

Two shop girls stood nearby, chatting in staccato phrases, totally oblivious to our presence. They quickly finished their coffee and relinquished their place at the bar. As they walked out of the café, Wendy remarked, "Very smart. Did you notice the short girl? I wonder where she found that blouse and scarf."

"Haven't we had this conversation before?" I asked.

"Probably." She ignored my attempt to change the subject. "The French have such a flair for just the right detail. Nothing pretentious, just the subtle little touch that can change the drab to the elegant."

I tried another tack. "Why is it that the French can take two hours for a leisurely lunch, yet begrudge two minutes for breakfast?"

She set down her coffee cup with a finality I recognized. "Let's see the shops on Saint-Honoré."

"I'd rather see the Musée d'Orsay."

"Too early," she replied. "We can do that later and have lunch there."

The rue Fauborgue Saint-Honoré shopping area is mercifully small, three short blocks from the rue Royal to the British Embassy, but it bears some of the proudest names of French couture. The windows are done with such imagination and taste that even I must agree that a few moments strolling there is time well spent. The danger is in the temptation to enter the shops, where more than time may be spent. The entrance to the British

Embassy serves as a mundane period, ending the statement made by the flashy windows.

Lunch at the Musée d'Orsay provides a lavish buffet at a modest price, and the ease with which we got a fine meal was in sharp contrast to our experiences on our first trip abroad. Then, arrangements had been made through a travel agent for us to celebrate our twentieth wedding anniversary with Christmas in London and New Year's in Paris. I would have been content with two weeks in English-speaking London rather than wasting time in a city where they ate frogs and spoke an unintelligible language, but Wendy had taken French in college and, succumbing to the brainwashing of her instructor, had developed an unrequited desire to see Paris.

We found London to be an exciting city, and we happily explored the British Museum, the National Galleries, the Tate, Trafalgar Square, the Tower and Buckingham Palace; in short, we saw everything that a tourist must see in our first two days. Then the city closed like a clam, withdrawing into an impenetrable shell for Christmas-Eve Day, Christmas Day, and then a third day, called Boxing Day. Of the six days we had allotted to London, three had been snatched away, and we were reduced to prowling the vacant streets in search of the few restaurants too poor to afford a holiday closing. Through the good offices of our travel agent, we were locked into a prepaid reservation system that precluded any adjustments.

When we arrived in France we were still fuming over the travel agent's failure to inform us about the holiday closures in England, but all was immediately forgiven when we received our first view of Paris from the hotel window. On the lower slopes of Montparnasse, our hotel commanded a sweeping view from the domes of Sacré Coeur to the spire of Notre Dame, with the Eiffel

Tower spotlighted between. A dull, smoky, late-afternoon sky reflected the nascent glow of the city.

A tiny park across the street was suddenly illuminated by a thousand crystal lights that traced the barren branches of each tree, while beyond the park, atop a tall building, a neon display flashed comets and starbursts above the words "Au Bon Marché."

"What does it say?" I asked.

"I think it's the name of a store."

"I think it means 'Welcome to Paris.'"

Wendy squeezed my hand, and we stood, transfixed for a moment. "Let's go walking," she said.

Alongside the hotel, street vendors had banked the snow against boxes of oysters, clams, and whelks, each with a sign giving the place of origin and the price. Seaweed decorated the boxes, releasing a pungent, salty aroma that teased the nose and conjured visions of the rock-bound coast from which the shellfish had been pried. On the corner, a flower stand was competing for the attention of the passing crowds, but judging from the flow of passersby it appeared flowers were an afterthought to the oysters in the shoppers' minds.

We walked along the park toward the building with the neon sign, stopping only to purchase a bag of roasted chestnuts from a man tending a charcoal fire burning within an old oil drum on wheels. I singed my fingers peeling the first and then proceeded to burn my tongue as I tasted the creamy paste within the shell. I suddenly realized that I was ravenously hungry. The bright lights of a small café beckoned to us. Within moments we were seated, and Wendy was perusing the short menu. She ordered, "*Crème caramel*," and held up two fingers to avoid any mistakes as she added, "*Deux*."

We ate the two little oval custards with their sugary sauce. I looked hungrily at the couple next to us who were consuming an enormous platter of french fries. Wendy was quick to interpret my glance. "Just a snack," she explained. "We don't want to spoil our dinner at the hotel."

I was content to let her take charge. After all, she had studied French, and I couldn't understand anything beyond *"Parlez-vous Français?"* which of course was no help. Nearly everyone at our hotel spoke English, making it easy at dinner for us to order fish, chicken, sausage and sauerkraut, or roast pork. It wasn't until we had repeatedly eaten *crème caramel* each day for lunch that I asked why we didn't have something different.

Wendy confessed, "*Crème caramel* is the only thing on the menu that I can pronounce."

Despite our linguistic deficiencies, Paris was a wonderland of delights. We bought a large map of the Métro and packets of tickets that allowed us access to every part of the city. We braved the icy wind to walk through the Tuileries gardens from the Place Concorde to the Louvre; we watched a black cat making tracks in the white snow beneath the even whiter domes of Sacré Coeur; we had what amounted to a private showing of the impressionist paintings at the Jeu de Paume on a day so blustery that few people were out. We even felt competent to discuss the relative merits of the neoclassical architecture of the Madeleine as compared to the Gothic grandeur of Notre Dame. In short, we had made Paris our own.

We were awakened on New Year's Day by the unbelievably loud ringing of the bedside telephone. Still groggy from the previous night's celebration with champagne and a Grand Marnier soufflé, I was hardly prepared for any surprises.

"Monsieur Thompson?" the heavily accented voice inquired.

"*Oui,*" I instinctively answered, the result of five days' orientation. Unfortunately, I had expended my entire vocabulary with that one word which the caller took as signal to continue in French.

It wasn't until he paused for breath that I was able to break in. "I'm sorry, but I didn't understand a word you said."

Wendy was now fully awake. "What's wrong?"

"Obscene phone call, I think. Can't really tell, though; it's in French." She moved closer, trying to hear as the voice shifted into English.

"Of course," he said. "You are American; I should have known to speak English." His tone was unmistakably condescending. "This is the desk manager. We would like to know at what time today you plan to check out."

"Check out? Today?" Wendy was clutching my shoulder and I almost dropped the telephone. "There must be some mistake. Our flight doesn't leave until tomorrow."

"Just one moment, please." I could hear the sound of papers being shuffled, then, "I am sorry Monsieur Thompson, your voucher is for 27 December to 31 December. That means that you check out on 1 January, which is today."

"Couldn't it be arranged for us to stay another day?"

I could almost hear him chuckle as he said, "But of course. I will put you down for another night."

The reason for his glee became apparent the following day when the bill was presented. Seven of our remaining fifty-dollar traveler's checks were put through the hotel's exchange machine, which extracted an additional ten percent and returned a twenty-franc note and some coins to us. Standing in that hotel lobby, frustrated and angry, I swore two oaths: 1. Learn enough French to order something besides *crème caramel*, and 2. Strangle that travel agent.

A couple of semesters of conversational French at our community college served to discharge the demands of the first oath. The second was never fulfilled. Rather than killing the man, we dispensed with his services and thus began a series of sojourns to

Europe, wholly independent of both travel agents and hotel reservations.

We traveled by train, air, and bus, but found that renting a car allowed us the most freedom to enjoy a town like Ornans—where Corot painted the landscapes which set the stage for the impressionists—rather than waste time at some souvenir shop chosen by a tour guide.

Perhaps I am too harsh in my judgment of guided tours; millions of people enjoy travel within the protective cocoon of a carefully planned itinerary, complete with reservations and a guide, to the extent that they are eager to repeat the experience. For those who need to know where they will sleep each night or are afraid of missing the outstanding attractions in each major city, I must concede that the guided tour is the most efficient means to accomplish their goals. These are the people who will find all of their fears about independent travel confirmed in this book. Those with a free spirit and a sense of humor, who have tried the guided tour and found it lacking, will find in this book a confirmation that independent travel in Europe is not only easy, but more fun.

Remember the fable about the farm dog and the wolf? The hungry wolf envied the well-fed dog until he saw the chain around the dog's neck and realized the price one must pay for security. Since the day Mark Twain published *Innocents Abroad*, perhaps a thousand guidebooks have been produced to tell a confused and fearful public exactly how to see Europe. This is not one of them. This book does not tell you how to do anything, although there is an appendix of helpful travel hints for those who insist on such things.

But why a book on France? Why not England, or Germany, or Italy? Because, in our experience, in no other foreign land will you find such diversity of landscape and people, coupled with such consistent friendliness as you will find in France. To the north, the peninsula of Brittany thrusts into the cold Channel waters which yield some of the best seafood in the world. The people here are of Celtic ancestry, and the ancient stone circles of the Druids are scattered throughout the land like miniature Stonehenges. Northeast of Brittany lies Normandy, an early conquest by the Norsemen, who found the land so appealing that they decided to stay. Further east, the ancient dukedoms of Picardy and Burgundy reflect the influence of the Germanic tribes who settled here before the time of Caesar. Throughout this area north of the Massif Central, one is aware of a quickness of speech, a restlessness of spirit that gets things done quickly and properly.

South of the Massif Central, life takes on a more leisurely pace, reflecting its ties to the Mediterranean cultures. Here you will see Cro-Magnon cave paintings, as well as the aqueducts, temples, and circuses that were built when the Roman Empire was at its apogee. Here, too, sitting like a glittering buckle at the foot of France, is the glitzy Riviera, famous for its beaches and abandonment to a hedonistic lifestyle that would be totally inappropriate in Brittany.

But with all its diversity, there are many constants in this country. Food, and its preparation, has been elevated to celebrity status in France, and a visit to the restaurant of a three-star chef is considered by many to be reason enough for a trip. It has been claimed that one cannot get a bad meal in France, although some of the new chain hotels and fast-food establishments along the major freeways are doing their best to disprove the statement. Supermarkets are common in the larger towns throughout France, but the local bakeries and delicatessens are holding their own. If you are planning to picnic, these *boulangeries* and *charcuteries* will provide the basis for some wonderful meals.

I was like a child given keys to the toy store on my first visit to a village *boulangerie*. We needed a baguette for a picnic, an easy task for one who had taken two semesters of conversational French. I was prepared linguistically, but totally unprepared emotionally for the subtle seduction that began with the first inhalation of the yeasty aroma and continued through a panoply of visual delights. I ended up buying a dark, crusty round of peasant bread and a half-dozen poppy seed rolls in addition to the baguette for which I had come.

Wendy's looked questioningly at the peasant loaf, but she immediately ate one of the rolls and said nothing about my profligacy. At the *charcuterie*, the visual display was even more captivating than at the bakery. Not just *pâté*, but *pâté* with truffles, *pâté* with olives, *pâté* with mushrooms, *pâté* in gelatin, and even a *pâté* with leeks.

We passed on the *pâté* and bought a generous slice of chicken *galantine*—boned, stuffed chicken poached and pressed into a loaf form. It would have been enough until I saw the *terrine de lapin*, coarse chopped meat with celery and sweet peppers set in gelatin. We added a slice to our order. Next, a bit of cheese and wine seemed in order, so we were off to the *épicier*. We were beginning to understand how the French think about food.

Language has always been a challenge, although you can get along quite well with a minimal vocabulary when it is accompanied by gestures, such as pointing to your choices on a menu. However, major confusions may arise when one assumes to know the meaning of a French word because it looks very much like an English word. You will see the word *Libre* prominently displayed on shop windows throughout France. Easy to guess that it should mean something about liberty and freedom, but nothing is free; the word is used to indicate self-service.

On a trip to explore Brittany and Normandy, we were happily settled in for a couple of days of leisurely sightseeing in Rouen, not far from the magnificent cathedral whose various aspects were so distinctively captured by Monet. However, our tranquility was rudely interrupted by the appearance of a sign on our hotel door, which read: *On Demande Femme de Chambre*. Although Wendy was generally accepting of French attitudes toward sex, this was too much! A woman in your chamber on demand? Absolutely not! We wasted the better part of a morning discussing whether we should find new lodgings. Only after we took the time to check *Larousse's* French-English dictionary did we find that *demande* has a much softer meaning in French: request. It seems that we had taken offense at a notice offering chambermaid service.

Later on the same trip, while driving the perimeter road along the coast of Brittany, I saw a sign that advertised *Plage Sauvage*, with an arrow pointing to a path which led into the sandy dunes. I pulled off into a parking area, fortunately sheltered by some trees, for the day was hot despite a few puffy clouds in the sky. Wendy looked dubiously at the path as she contemplated the sandy walk ahead.

"I think I'll stay in the car and nap," she said. "You enjoy the savage beach; the last thing I need is sand in my shoes."

I went on alone. Visions of monstrous waves crashing against a rocky shore, while gulls and stormy petrels screamed their defiance to the savage elements, kept me plodding along, with only an occasional stop to dump the sand from my shoes. I pushed my way through tall sea grasses, clinging tenuously to their sandy hillocks, until I could hear the whispery sound of the surf. One last surge over the highest dune and I was in sight of the ocean. Confusingly, the beach lay flat and smooth, and the waves were no more than a foot high as they gently swept onto the sand. There were no rocks, no birds, only a few languid sunbathers stretched stark naked before my startled gaze. *Sauvage*, in this case, meant back to nature, and there I stood, fully clothed.

Never have I felt so naked as I did that day in the presence of those unclothed bodies.

Each year we returned from Europe with new experiences and understanding, to be faced with the same old question, "How can you afford it? We hear that it's so expensive." Expensive? Yes, when compared to staying home, but when compared to other vacations, going to France needn't be more expensive than a trip to Mexico or Florida, and may be less than Washington, D.C., or New York. Air fare is the single expense that is beyond the traveler's control, but even here, by carefully choosing a charter flight, costs can be held to a minimum. Once in France, if the major cities are avoided, prices will seem to be surprisingly low.

Hotels in Paris and the Riviera can be terribly expensive, with rates beginning at $400 per day, but even in those areas, if you are willing to forgo the luxury of having your bed covers turned back for you, reasonable accommodations can be found. In Paris, numerous small hotels offer rooms for $100 or less, but no travel agent will list them. To find them, we recommend spending a few hours walking in an area of the city you like. You won't even have to ask about the rates—they are posted in the lobbies for all to see. (It doesn't hurt to make reservations for your first night, then to go out and do your scouting secure in the knowledge that you'll have a bed to fall back into. Yes, I did say "reservations," but Paris is the only city in France for which we make this exception. After an exhausting trans-Atlantic flight, finding a room in this bustling city can be more than a little daunting.)

The Riviera is a bit trickier. However, in the hills above the crowded resorts there are numerous ancient towns with affordable lodgings and sweeping views of the Mediterranean, and some of the hotels will even have restaurants. An early start is recommended because these are small hotels with limited space, and the best are filled well before sundown. Once situated, you can sweep down to join the crowds on the beach, happy in the knowledge that you have not only a room with a view, but that you are paying only a fraction of what the rest are. Don't stay at the beach too long, however, for there are no street lights on the roads into the hills and few landmarks to guide you in the dark. A lost hotel is worse than no hotel at all.

An example of what we've found in the hills overlooking the Mediterranean was a little hotel at Camp du Garde which occupied one of the five buildings that make up the town. There, four of us enjoyed a substantial dinner with wine, a night's lodging and *le petit déjeuner* for slightly less than a hundred francs, or about eight dollars per person at the then-prevailing exchange rate. Even if the price has quadrupled since then, it would still be a bargain.

Another example, far to the north, was a hotel at Vaucouleurs, one of the many towns claiming to be the birth place of Jeanne d'Arc. There, two of us relished a seven-course dinner and a sound night's lodging for only ninety francs, or about thirty dollars. You will note that the translation into U.S. dollars will vary over time, anywhere from three francs to the dollar to eight, but the bargains remain. A ten-percent revaluation of the dollar will hardly be noticed if you are paying only fifty dollars for a room.

On the other hand, electricity costs five times as much in France as it does in the United States, and the French will go to great lengths to conserve it. Hotels will claim air conditioning when only the lobby is cooled; if individual rooms are equipped with cooling units, the price of the room will be at least fifty dollars more than a similar room without a unit. Timing devices on lights are universal in hotel hallways. You push the little glowing button and the lights come on, but only for the length of time it takes to find your room and unlock the door. Dawdlers are doomed to darkness.

Electricity is not the only energy source that is high priced in Europe. All fuel is expensive, and its cost is the second-biggest worry for Americans considering footloose travel by rental car. Actually, if you rent a small car, without the luxury of air conditioning, you will be surprised at how little gasoline it takes to get you wherever you want to go. Our automobile costs, including gasoline and insurance, have averaged between thirty-five and forty dollars a day. Cheaper rental rates are often available through a tie-in with an airline, but little can be done about the cost of fuel. A tip worth remembering is to refuel on the outskirts of large cities rather than on the open road, where lack of competition can lead to higher prices.

Our trips, generally of a two-week duration, will usually cost between four and five thousand dollars for us both, including air fare. The major variable is always the number of days spent in large cities. A single day in Paris will cost as much as three or four days in the hinterland, but it can be worth it.

Either way, without reservations, the choice is yours.

~ On Your Own ~

In this section, you will find listings of recommended accommodations, restaurants, and additional points of interest, along with a general idea of the costs involved. Remember that all prices are subject to change, and although the costs quoted were accurate at the time of publication, there may be some variation at a later date—use them simply as a rough guide to relative value. Also, since it is not possible to accurately forecast the exchange rate between the French franc and the U.S. dollar, a five-for-one rate has arbitrarily been used to translate prices, i.e. 5F = $1.

Transportation

As far as getting to France goes, we usually fly on a major, scheduled airline, using what is termed an **APEX fare**. While this requires a minimum stay of fourteen days and costs a bit more than a chartered flight, it allows for a flexibility unavailable on charter flights.

A **taxi** ride from Charles de Gaulle Airport into the city will cost about $40 and take you directly to your hotel. Two or three people may share a taxi; a fourth will cost extra. You will need French money to pay—if the taxi driver is willing to accept foreign currency, it will be at the most disadvantageous rate possible. It's best to change a hundred dollars at the airport window after you pass through customs.

Less expensive transportation is available: the **Air France bus** will take you to central Paris for about $8 per person. This will entail the additional cost of a taxi to your hotel from the bus terminal as well as the transfer of your luggage from the bus to the taxi. After a long flight, the last thing I want is to worry about luggage. For me, eliminating the hassle factor is worth the extra $15 to $20.

Once in Paris you will find the **Métro** system to be both economical and convenient. A single ticket costs about one dollar and will allow you to go anywhere in Paris by either bus or underground train. Free maps are available at Métro stations and provide easily understood information, including the number of each bus stopping at any destination. A packet of ten tickets will cost about $6 and may be purchased at tobacco stores (Tabac) as well as Métro stations. Tickets are validated when you begin your ride and must be retained until you are off the vehicle. Failure to produce a validated ticket, when requested, will result in a fine on the spot. I have never been asked, but the possibility of a fine keeps me hanging on to the ticket. Some lines carry passengers beyond the city limits into the suburbs. For those destinations, you will need two or even three tickets. Check with the driver.

Paris

It seems almost impertinent to discuss Paris in a footnote. Undoubtedly more books have been written about Paris than any other city in the world. With this in mind, I have attempted to provide a few recommendations of things to do and see which you are not likely to find in most guidebooks.

Attractions

For those not familiar with Paris, a two-hour bus tour on **Cityrama** is recommended. Although it may seem expensive at 145F (about $29), it will provide a comfortable orientation to the city's layout, with individual earphones providing a commentary in English as you pass by such legendary sights as Notre-Dame, the Eiffel Tower, and the Louvre.

Tours begin at 9:30 am. The bus terminal is at #4, place des Pyramides. Any taxi driver will know it, or you can take the Métro to the Tuilleries Station.

It is assumed that you will have seen the Louvre and the Musée d'Orsay, but while you are in the same area, don't miss the **Musée de l'Orangerie des Tuileries,** located just up the stairway from the Place de la Concorde. Here you will see Monet's *Nymphéas* (water lilies) as well as paintings by Renoir, Cézanne, Rousseau, Picasso, Utrillo, and many others. Admission is 26F (about $5) for adults, but free for children under 18. Closed Tuesdays, the museum is otherwise open from 9:45 am to 5:15 pm. It may be easily reached via the Métro by getting off at the Concorde Station. Phone: 42-97-48-16.

While visiting the Cathédrale Notre-Dame de Paris and Louis IX's private chapel on the Ile de la Cité, Sainte Chapelle, set aside an extra hour to see **La Conciergerie.** You can't mistake its entrance, set between the twin 14th-century towers, the Tour d'Argent and the Tour de César. Originally built as a palace for kings, its vast dining hall was transformed into a "peoples' court" during the Revolution, where justice was pronounced against nobility. Here were heard the pitiful cries of Marie Antoinette, imprisoned while she awaited trial. Other notables who passed through this dark place on their way to the guillotine included Madame du Barry and even such leaders of the Revolution as Danton and Robespierre. Admission is 31F (about $6) for adults, with a special fee of 16F (about $3) for those over 60. Open daily from 10:00 am to 5:00 pm. It's easily reached from Métro Stations Cité or Châtelet. Phone: 43-54-30-06.

The **Hôtel Carnavalet,** on rue de Sévigné near the Place des Vosges, provides an intimate glimpse of France as it bathed in the blood of the Revolution. Built in 1544, the Hôtel was remodeled by Francois Mansart in 1661 to become the home of Madame de Sévigné (famous for her letters to La Rochefoucauld) and was acquired for a museum by the city in 1866. Here you will see such items as the chess set used by Louis XVI to pass his time in confinement while awaiting his appointment with the guillotine. More touching is the school workbook of the little Dauphin who disappeared so mysteriously. In yet another room you will find the original of the *Declarations of the Rights of Man and the Citizen,* along with orders of execution and models of the guillotine. Other rooms contain maps, flags, bric-a-brac, and models of Paris designed to show its evolution. Paintings abound; not to be missed is the Bouvier collection on the first floor. Admission is 30F (about $6) for adults, but only 20F ($4) for those over 60. Hours are 10:00 am to 5:40 pm, closed on Mondays. Take the Métro to St-Paul Station. Phone: 42-72-21-13.

The **Musée de Cluny** is one of the oldest examples of medieval architecture in Paris. The original mansion was built over the ruins of a Roman bath from the days of Tiberius. More important than the architecture, however, is the collection of arts and crafts from the Middle Ages, probably the finest to be seen anywhere. Included in the collection are the six Unicorn Tapestries, famous throughout the world for their depiction of a beautiful princess surrounded by her handmaidens, pets, and fanciful animals. Also, you will see the statues that originally adorned the king's chamber of Sainte Chapelle, along with various gem-studded crosses, cups of gold, ivory carvings, and assorted vestments from 12th- and 13th-century churches. Admission is 17F (about $4) with no discount for age, although on Sundays the charge is only 9F ($2). The museum is closed Tuesdays. Take the Métro to Cluny Station. Phone: 43-25-62-00.

Lest you think Paris is only a vast conglomeration of museums and monuments, a day spent at **La Cité des Sciences et de l'Industrie** will demonstrate that Parisians are enamored with the present and future as well as the past. Set in the Parc de la Villette is a glass and stainless-steel building of such enormous proportions that it could easily be a hangar for the spaceship from the movie *Star Wars*. The interior contains three levels of rotating exhibits and several permanent exhibits. Here you will be amazed to see a full-scale planetarium and a geodesic dome that houses a 370-seat, 3-D cinema. All exhibits and the restaurant have wheelchair access. Admission is 45F (about $9), which covers all exhibits, but not the theatre (it costs an additional 50F to take in the show at the Geode). Closed Mondays, the hall is open from 10 am to 6 pm, except on Wednesdays, Saturdays, Sundays, and holidays, when it opens at noon. To compensate for the late openings, on those days the exhibits remain open until 8 pm. Take the Métro to La Villette Station. Phone: 40-05-80-00.

Hotels

Paris is one of the most expensive cities in the world, and hotel rates are priced accordingly. However, it is possible to find centrally located hotels which are both clean and pleasant, yet priced at $100-150 for a double room with bath or shower. Expect the rooms to be small, and don't look for valet and room service. Paris is the one city in France where *advance reservations are a must, and it is a good idea to send a deposit for the first night. The following list will give you some idea of what is available. All prices are for double accommodations.*

Near the Champs-Élysées (the most popular/expensive area)

The **Galileo Hôtel** (54, rue Galilée, 75008 Paris) is not only conveniently located, but is also recently remodeled. Rates: 950-1000F ($190-200). Phone: 47-20-66-06.

The **Lord Byron** (5, rue de Châteaubriand, 75008 Paris), charmingly furnished with antiques, is a quiet place to rest after a day of touring. Rates: 800-900F ($160-180). Phone: 43-59-89-98.

Near the Madeleine, Opéra, and Place Concorde

The **Lido** (4, passage de la Madeleine, 75008 Paris) is also quiet and, as a member of Best Western International, allows for convenient booking from the U.S., if you so desire. Rates: 800-900F ($160-180). Phone: 42-66-61-23. Best Western International: 1-800-528-1234.

The **Madeleine-Plaza** (33, place de la Madeleine, 75008 Paris) is very reasonably priced, but noisy, unless you book an interior room. Rates: 400-470F ($80-95). Phone: 42-65-20-63.

In the Latin Quarter (the famous Left Bank student/artist area)

Élysa-Luxembourg (6, rue Gay-Lussac, 75005 Paris) is located near the Jardin du Luxembourg and is a haven of quiet. Rates: 560-700F ($110-140). Phone: 43-25-31-74.

In Montmartre

The **Hôtel New Montmartre** (7, rue Paul-Albert, 75018 Paris) is only about a block from Sacré-Coeur. Rates: 580F ($115). Phone: 46-06-03-03.

Restaurants

Eating is serious business for the French, and they treat dining out at a restaurant as we would an evening at a show or concert. For the casual diner, brasseries, cafés, and bistros all serve food of varying excellence. Here reservations are not generally required, and the first-come, first-served rule applies. But this is not so at proper restaurants. For these, reservations are a must, sometimes months in advance for those rating the Michelin three stars. The restaurants listed below have not yet reached that lofty designation and are more likely to be able to seat you with only a few days' notice. If the wine list intimidates you, don't hesitate to order a carafe of house wine. It is usually quite good and much cheaper than those on la carte des vins.

Near the Champs-Élysées

La Boutique a Sandwiches (12, rue du Colisée) serves imaginative sandwiches, with *plat du jour* dishes available. Even here, reservations are needed. Open 11:45 am to 1:00 am, but closed Sundays and all of August. Menus: 75-150F ($15-30) per person. Phone: 43-59-56-69.

Chez Edgard (4, rue Marbeuf) is popular with the locals and worth a try. There is an outside terrace, but most customers prefer the red-and-black Belle Epoque interior. Lunch noon-3:00 pm, dinner 7:00 pm-12:30 am, closed Sundays. Menus: 250-500F ($50-100), depending upon the wine. Phone: 47-20-51-15.

Near the Madeleine

At **Le 30/Chez Fauchon** (30, place de la Madeleine), if your mouth has been watering from looking in display windows, here is where you'll get your chance to try some of Paris' delectables. Lunch 12:15-2:30 pm, dinner 7:30-10:30 pm, closed Sundays. Menus: 300-400F ($60-80). Phone: 47-42-56-58.

Near the Opéra

Goumard (17, rue Duphot) specializes in fresh seafood. Closed on Sundays and for vacations during the second week of August and over the Christmas holidays. Menus: 300-500F ($60-100), including a bottle of wine. Phone: 42-96-20-70.

Near the Louvre

La Moisanderie (52, rue de Richelieu) has small tables crammed into a tiny space that quickly fills with people eager for the excellent food at reasonable prices. Open for dinner from 7:00 to 10:30 pm, closed Sundays. Menus: 110-220F ($20-45). Phone: 42-96-92-93.

Near Les Invalides

Chez les Anges (54, blvd. de Latour-Maubourg) specializes in the dishes of Burgundy, including calves' liver which is cooked very rare. I have tried to avoid restaurants which specialize in exotic dishes such as tripe, calves' liver, and brains, and although such things will appear on menus, at least Chez les Anges does not specialize in such things! Try their *boeuf bourguignon* instead. Open for dinner 7:00-11:00 pm, closed Sundays. Menus: 250-400F ($50-80) with wine. Phone: 47-05-89-86.

Nuit de Saint Jean (29, rue Surcouf) feels more like a café than a restaurant, containing only enough room to seat 30 people. Specializing in the cuisine of Aquitaine, it features cassoulet, lamb curry, chicken marinated in lime juice, and fish cooked in a champagne-cream sauce. Open for dinner 7:30-10:30 pm, closed Sundays. Menus: 150-200F ($30-40), if you drink the house wine. Phone: 45-51-61-49.

In Montparnasse

Le Ciel de Paris (33, ave. du Maine) is located in a monstrous office tower which covers an entire block here in the Left Bank's Montparnasse. Most visitors pay 35.50F (about $7) for a ride to the 56th-floor observation deck for the panoramic views, but your ride to the restaurant is free. After dinner, when you settle your check, ask the waiter for a free pass to the observation deck; it stays open until 11:00 pm from April through October, but closes at 10:00 pm during the winter months. Menus: 250F ($50). Phone: 45-38-52-35.

Cafes, Bistros, and Nightlife

For those on a nostalgia kick for popular French music of the thirties, **Le Caveau des Oubliettes** (11, rue St-Julien-le-Pauvre—take the Métro to station St-Michel) is made to order. Drinks are expensive, but the beautifully sung *chansons* are well worth the price. Open nightly, 9:00 pm to 2:00 am. Phone: 45-83-41-77. Cash only.

Also, in the same general Left Bank area is **Le Caveau de la Bolée** (25, rue de l'Hirondelle). The programs are still mostly *chansons*, but some evenings are given over to jazz. Prices are lower than at des Oubliettes, and the crowd is younger. Open nightly, 9:30 pm until 6:30 am. Phone: 43-54-62-20.

If your preference is for more modern music, **Les Alligators'** (23, ave. du Maine) large stage features well-known French and international jazz bands. While there is no admission or cover charge, your first drink will set you back 140F ($28). Subsequent drinks are cheaper, but the piper must be paid. Open 10:00 pm to 4:00 am, closed Sundays. Phone: 42-84-11-27.

For something a little less sophisticated and much less costly, try **Le Petit Journal** (71, blvd. St-Michel—use the Métro Luxembourg). Here in a tiny, smoky bar you will hear talented but largely unknown musicians play all manner of jazz, even Dixieland. Open 10:00 pm to 2:00 am, closed Sundays. Phone: 43-26-28-59.

If you want something really different, stop in at **Le Tango** (13, rue Au-Maire). Looking slightly worn now, this dance hall has been in operation for nearly a century. Drinks are cheap and no one will judge your style, so give it a whirl. Open Wednesday through Saturday nights from 11:00 pm until 5:00 am. Phone: 48-87-54-78.

If you thought France was for wine snobs, try a meal at one of Paris' many "beer cellars" for good food and a taste of some of the world's finest brews. Recommended: **La Gueuze** at 19, rue Soufflot (Métro Luxembourg) and **Gambrinus** at 62, rue des Lombards (Métro Châtelet-Les-Halles). If you insist on wine, try one of the following wine bars: **Le Rubis** at 10, rue du Marché-St-Honoré (Métro Station Pyramides) and **La Tartine** at 24, rue de Rivoli (Métro Station St-Paul).

Chapter 2

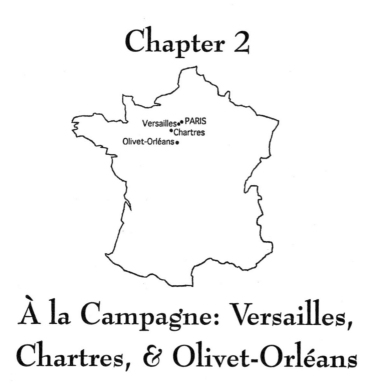

Versailles•• PARIS
•Chartres
Olivet-Orléans•

À la Campagne: Versailles, Chartres, & Olivet-Orléans

The lopsided, three-quarter moon hung like a silver balloon above the truncated towers of Notre Dame as we glided by on the sightseeing boat. Dinner had elegantly contradicted the implication of the name *Bateau Mouche*—boat of flies. On the reception deck we were offered an apéritif of champagne laced with a dash of Poire William, setting us in a festive mood while the boat loaded the remaining passengers. Delicate harp strains wafted around the deck with the evanescence of snowflakes in summer as we were escorted to our table. The five-course dinner that followed was accompanied by two bottles of wine, one white, one red, for each couple, and they served to gradually loosen the social strictures which earlier had kept the passengers isolated strangers. Following dinner, an accordion player replaced the harpist, and we joined other couples on the dance floor, amid laughter and a bantered babble of assorted languages. We had become kin, tourists all, as we floated harmoniously down the Seine, the illuminated splendor of Paris slipping by.

The enchantment of that night carried over to the following morning when we began an excursion, by Métro, to Vincennes, the medieval residence of the French royalty. The ride was fast and smooth, on a train equipped with rubber tires like those of an automobile, and the final leg was above ground where we could see stretches of small houses interspersed among high-rise apartments.

The train stopped at Cours de Vincennes, a hot and dusty little enclave of old buildings surrounding a square which featured the statues of two forgotten kings atop high pedestals. Off in the distance to the left, we could see a mammoth building sprawled across a slight hill, not the elegant palace we had expected. Straight ahead, a small grove of trees promised the only possible shade on a day which was rapidly warming. We thought we were beginning to see why the Bois de Vincennes was not featured in many travel guides.

The crowd from the train, mostly mothers with small children, had rapidly dispersed along a crossroad, following a sign pointing the way to a zoo. As we approached, Wendy studied the sign as though she intended to memorize the phrase *Jardin Zoologique*, then fixed me with a steady gaze. "We have to talk." There seemed nothing to do but find a place in the shade where we could get a cold drink. Last night's enchantment was obviously gone.

"We didn't fly all the way over here to see a zoo," she began, "and from what I can see of the château, it looks even less interesting."

"We could get a car and drive into the country."

Her face brightened. "May I pick where we go?" This was a not-too-subtle reminder that Vincennes had been my idea.

"Of course, as long as we agree on some simple rules." The basic idea of getting out into the country was great, but memories of other such excursions suggested some cautionary guidelines. "First, we drive no more than two hours without a break."

She nodded acceptance. "It'll give us plenty of time to explore."

"Second, we travel back roads as much as possible, never traveling on a high-speed *péage*; and third, we find a place for the night before 4:00 in the afternoon."

"You'll be driving, so it all sounds fine to me." She then proceeded to summarize the rules in more positive terms. "A two-hour drive would put us somewhere in time for lunch, and if we stopped by 4:00 pm, we should have no trouble in finding a good hotel, with time left for exploring before dinner." Wendy was really getting caught up in the spirit. "As for the *péage*, what's the purpose of driving into the country if you just whisk from one big city to another? Give me the good old country roads any time."

"Where would you like to go?" I asked.

Wendy thought for a moment. "Remember that cute little place we stayed in years ago in Vence? I wonder if it's still there. And we could see the Matisse Chapel and the Maight Museum. I don't much care about seeing St. Paul de Vence again, though...too commercial."

"That would be okay for tomorrow. I meant right now." I indicated the wooded park around us with a sweep of the hand. "We're here. We might as well see the place."

"I think we've seen it, but a little walk can't hurt." She stood and quickly began walking in the direction opposite the path to the zoo. "Are you coming?"

With negative expectations, we strolled into the woods, totally unprepared for the sudden appearance of a massive planting of dahlias of every description and color. Tall and short, they were banked around a large building which blocked our view until we rounded its corner. Ahead lay another structure called the "Exotarium," which was a combination aquarium and snake house. We passed it by for the more appealing lake, its well-tended, sandy shores planted with weeping willows and Lombardy poplars. Various breeds of ducks floated on the tranquil surface, to be joined by a single snow-white swan as we watched. Several pavilions, resembling enlarged 19th-century gazebos, made a rough semi-circle around a formal garden area. Stubby boxwood hedges separated the plots in a geometric design, and across the plantings, the umbrellas on a terrace proclaimed the presence of a restaurant.

"It's too early for lunch," Wendy said, reading my thoughts. "Let's see the château and come back."

"Thought you'd seen enough."

She ignored my remark and continued, "This is so beautiful. Makes me wonder how many things we've passed by because the first impression wasn't great." She took my arm and led me up the path toward the castle, which looked more impressive the closer we got. The towers of the keep loomed ahead, looking like massive, stone, grain elevators, except for the embrasures.

After wandering around the château for an hour or so, we returned to the gardens and the restaurant. Over a couple of *croque-monsieur*, a French version of a grilled ham-and-cheese sandwich, and a *pichet* of red wine, Wendy resumed our conversation about the pending auto trip. "I want to go to Albi. We must go to Albi. That's where we saw the Maurice Utrillo exhibit, remember?"

"I thought you wanted to go to Vence."

"Of course I do. Can't we do both?"

I visualized the map. Vence was over to the right, just above Nice on the Côte d'Azur, and Albi? It was way over to the left, almost to the Spanish border. The distance between the two would almost equal the distance from Paris to either one. The trip was taking on proportions far beyond a Sunday drive, and there seemed no reasonable way out of the bargain.

"Well," I began, hoping for a cancellation of one of her choices. "We could do sort of a large triangle, but we won't be able to stay in any one place for more than a day or two."

"That's all right. I enjoy driving through the countryside a whole lot more than poking around cities."

I knew when I was licked. "Okay, the great triangle tour it is."

The following morning we packed our bags and somehow jammed them, along with ourselves, into the tiny elevator at our hotel. Although we always think that we are traveling light—one suitcase and one carry-on bag each—the elevators in most French hotels seem to have been designed only for backpackers, and very skinny ones at that. Old Gray, the scruffy looking bag no self-respecting thief would steal, now bore the additional weight of travel books and sat uneasily upended in the corner. The other pieces were piled atop to form a precarious column. After a shuddering stop and a bruised ankle from the elevator door closing while I wrestled out Old Gray, we made it to the lobby. A few moments at the desk to check out and arrange for a taxi and we were on our way to the car rental office just off the Champs-Élysées.

The cab driver had seemed particularly smug as he threw our luggage into the trunk, although his smile faded somewhat when he hefted Old Gray. "Which airline?" he asked in a happy tone.

"No airline," I responded, trying to reflect his cheerful demeanor. "Champs-Élysées."

His smile faded and his shoulders slumped as the realization struck him. He had loaded all that luggage with only a twenty-franc fare in prospect instead of the two hundred and twenty francs he had anticipated. It was a surly man who dumped our bags on the curb. He hardly nodded to acknowledge the extra five francs I gave him for his trouble.

The car agency was located halfway through an arcade and, worse, down two flights of stairs. Wendy bounced ahead with the two carry-ons, leaving me to limp along like a drunken sailor with a ship's anchor in Old Gray. With the last of my strength, I heaved the suitcase through the doorway and stumbled along after in its wake.

"*L'ascenseur ne marche pas?*" questioned the man behind the desk.

I ignored his reference to an unknown elevator and asked if he spoke English.

"But, of course," he replied. "What service do you require?"

"We need a car, the smallest you have, for a week, maybe ten days."

He nodded happily and began filling out a form while I further explained that we wanted unlimited mileage and full insurance. The credit card company had assured me that insurance on car rentals was unnecessary, but there is comfort in knowing that any unexpected accidents will be fully covered. Furthermore, proof of insurance is needed in any accident where the police are involved, and the extra charge seems worth paying to avoid the potential of an international whirlwind of papers and red tape.

He accepted my credit card, made note of my driver's license and passport numbers, and after I had signed and initialed the rental agreement, he handed me a set of keys. "Your car is a new green Fiat on level five. You will see it directly in front of the elevator. Have a good trip."

"The elevator?" I questioned as I bent my knees, preparing to bench press Old Gray.

"To your left," he said and pointed to be sure I understood.

I picked up the baggage and staggered back through the door. Just as I exited, the agent called after me in a cheery tone, "You know, for ten francs we pick up and deliver the car to your hotel?" I pretended not to hear.

Our rental was a handy little two-door sedan, with ample room for all our bags in the trunk and a sporty five-on-the-floor transmission. After a few minutes of seat adjustments and trying out of the various controls, I turned the ignition key and the engine came to life. "Where away?" I smiled triumphantly.

"Seat belt first." Wendy reminded me that the French police can collect on-the-spot fines from motorists without seat belts. I buckled up. "Now, Versailles," Wendy continued. "We can make it in time for lunch."

The *autoroute* from Paris to Versailles is like a drive on a Los Angeles freeway. Everyone is in a hurry and lets you know that a casual tourist is not only a nuisance, but is expendable. Fortunately, the route is well marked with large blue signs indicating both direction and distance—well marked, that is, until the final turnoff, which is indicated only by a tiny white sign placed low by the roadside at the turn itself. Wendy's perceptions were keen, sharpened no doubt by the approaching lunch hour. She spotted the sign in time for me to signal and slow without being rear-ended by a particularly aggressive driver who was tailgating with the reckless abandon of a teenager on a skateboard.

The palace was easy enough to find, but parking was an entirely different matter. One hundred and seventy-three buses sat in the cobblestone lot, panting in the growing heat of the late morning as they maintained air-conditioned comfort for their clients. We drove slowly twice around the loop until we found a place under the shade of ancient elms. Parking meters in France deliver a time-stamped receipt which must be placed on the dashboard for easy visibility. Often the meter that dispenses the ticket is located on the opposite side of the street and as much as a half-block away. This time it was quickly found, and for a five-franc coin, we were assured an hour's tranquility for lunch.

We found an empty sidewalk table that faced the palace. Sheltered from the sun by an umbrella proclaiming the virtues of Stella Artois beer and cooled by an occasional puff of breeze, we settled down to a light lunch of chicken salad and fresh baguette, accompanied by a glass of steely cold muscadet. I shifted a foot beneath the table and idly considered the possibility that Marie Antoinette might have crossed that very spot. Unlikely, of course, that the young Queen's foot ever touched any "common" ground, but still a pleasant fancy.

We sat and munched and wondered what the scene would have looked like a few centuries earlier. The vast baroque facade seemed to brood over its faded glory, its windows no longer reflecting the splendor of gilded coaches drawn by plumed horses. The vista was, as always, lovely to behold, but having spent several days on previous trips exploring the extravagant palace and extensive gardens, we left Versailles to the bus tours and moved along.

The road from Versailles to Chartres was postcard perfect, with long, straight stretches edged with stately Lombardy poplars. The fields on either side were bounded by ancient walls of stone, maintained through the centuries by succeeding generations. Rows of green corn marched in orderly fashion over rounded hills, occasionally broken by brilliant splashes of yellow sunflowers. How strange, we thought, to see crops from America growing abundantly in fields which had been fenced off centuries before the continent was discovered.

What hands, we wondered, had laid the first stone of those enduring walls? Was it placed while Roman legions patrolled Gaul's countryside? What minds had directed the careful, patient placing of each successive layer so that it was firmly locked to the one below? It seems unlikely the wall-builders knew that they were creating monuments to the genius of man, as they brought order out of chaos. Or did they?

Such questions can never be answered, of course, but they serve to bind the mind of the traveler to the land traversed, providing memories more precious than answers could ever be.

We reached Chartres in the early afternoon, with the sun white hot in the hazy sky. Survival demanded replacement of moisture on such a day, so we sat down under an umbrella at the café nearest the cathedral. I ordered a beer, and Wendy had a bottle of grapefruit juice *avec glaçons*, probably relishing the ice cubes more than the juice.

Refreshed, but still limp from the heat, we made our way into the cathedral. No matter how often one has visited these magnificent achievements of medieval architects, the visual impact of those vaulted stone columns sweeping skyward is breathtaking. As the door closed behind us, we stood in the hushed gloom, waiting for our eyes to adjust, welcoming the cool air of the interior.

Begun after the first millennium, Chartres cathedral had taken three generations of craftsmen to cut and pile stone upon stone to form the framework for the glorious curtains of multicolored glass. We slowly walked down the aisle to the transept, studying each panel, reading the stories of saints and martyrs frozen for the second millennium in those luminous windows.

And then we looked back at the rose window, a window designed to tell no story, but to speak only of the eternal glory of God. That human minds had conceived and human hands had fashioned such radiant perfection would leave even a pagan in awe.

We spent far more time in the cathedral than we had intended, but it was time I shall always consider well spent. Our mistake was in deciding to drive all the way to Olivet, a small city just across the Loire River from Orléans, for that evening's lodgings. Although the sun was lower, it shone with punishing intensity, and the heat had not abated in the slightest. The fields along the road were beautiful within their boundaries of stone; the small villages, with their old stone houses decorated with pots of geraniums and marigolds, were quaint, yet they seemed different to us now. They had come to represent an impediment. The constant heat of the late afternoon had made us irritable, but worse than that, I felt victimized by that terrible concept of travel: a destination!

Three promising small hotels in Olivet turned us away with an apologetic "*C'est complet*," so in desperation we turned into the parking lot of a chain motel, a French attempt at duplicating the generic American corporate lodging. It would be pricey, we knew, but the feel of the air-conditioned lobby convinced us that, for this night at least, we would receive full value. We hefted our carry-on bags to our room on the second floor and flopped down on the bed, exhausted. Old Gray could spend the night in the car, for all I cared. "Let's not go out again," Wendy said with the finality of a command. "There's a restaurant here. It might be good."

The "restaurant" was named Le Grill and featured a limited selection that could have been copied from Denny's. A waiter proudly handed us the glossy, fold-out menus, printed in living color. Opening to the first fold, we were amused to find a listing of "Starters" where we had expected "hors d'oeuvres." We decided that this British usage must be a French concession to the

Common Market. We made our selections from the starter list: a green salad for Wendy and crudités from the buffet of raw vegetables for me. These were to be followed by the ubiquitous steak and *frites* for Wendy, while I chose the grilled lamb chops from the listing of entrées.

To accompany the food, we ordered a bottle of red Chinon, produced within a few miles of Orléans. The waiter indicated that I should go to the buffet for my crudités whenever I wished and then disappeared to fill our orders. I dallied for a moment, pending the arrival of the wine; I knew that the waiter would be displeased if I were not there for the ritual wine tasting. "Get your veggies," Wendy said, "then you'll be ready when they bring my salad." As I started to rise, a strange waiter dashed up to our table and, with a great flourish, placed a platter of steak and fried potatoes before Wendy. "No, no!" she protested. "My salad?"

The waiter looked perplexed. After all, had he not served the steak in the best American fast-food tradition? Wendy was adamant. "No," she repeated, "That can't be mine. You're not even our waiter!"

The waiter looked absolutely dejected as he withdrew the offending plate and returned it to the kitchen. A moment later, we were visited by a third person who seemed to be someone in authority. "There is some problem with your order?" he questioned.

"I wanted my salad first." Wendy said in a firm voice.

"Salad first?" The man was dumbfounded. French tradition calls for the salad to be served after the entrée. "Salad first?" he repeated, like a father to a child. It looked like a stand-off, but Wendy met his gaze with the unyielding look I knew so well. Finally, the man shrugged his shoulders. "As you wish." He stalked off.

"*Oui, la salade première et les viandes, ensuite,*" I said, practicing my French.

"Why didn't you say that when the man was here?" Wendy asked, a bemused smirk belying the innocence of her question.

"You had him licked, hands down. Besides, I couldn't think of the words soon enough."

Now, Wendy's salad appeared, delivered by yet another person, this one a woman of mature years who obviously had been selected as being capable of dealing with the crazy Americans. "*La salade pour Madame*," she explained.

"*Merci*," Wendy responded.

"*Le vin?*" I asked.

"*Desirez vous du vin?*"

"*Oui, une bouteille de Chinon rouge, s'il vous plaît.*" With that I exhausted my French and patience for the evening.

She looked confused, but most people do when I try out my French, so I thought little about it until a fifth person arrived with a bottle of wine bearing the label Saint Chinian, not Chinon. But it at least was red and would do. Particularly in light of the waitress' return with Wendy's steak and my lamb chops.

In all the confusion, I had forgotten to specify "*bien cuit*" when ordering Wendy's steak, so it arrived blood rare. "I can't eat this," she whispered.

We exchanged plates. The waitress said nothing.

"Aren't you going to get your crudités?" Wendy asked.

"*Ensuite*," I muttered, downing my first glass of Saint Chinian rouge in a single gulp.

Later, looking out the window of our room, across the darkening fields toward a row of hills on the horizon, I reflected on our first day *à la campagne*. Not all bad. We were fed and had shelter for the night, and we had seen some of the real France we remembered from our prior journeys, although it was difficult to reconcile such memories with the reality of Le Grill.

"Stop brooding and come to bed," Wendy invited, patting the place at her side.

"Right," I said. "But from now on, we stop driving at four o'clock."

"Yeah," she said, "right."

~ On Your Own ~

Versailles

Since Versailles is so close to Paris, you may choose to make your visit a one-day excursion, leaving your luggage in your Paris hotel. It's an easy trip by Métro bus #171 which you catch at Pont de Sèvres in Paris and which deposits you at the main gate of the palace. You will use three Métro tickets each way. The palace and grounds are closed on Mondays and national holidays.

Attractions

While the palace alone is a must-see for any tourist in France, there is much to see beyond the Grands Appartements and the fabled Hall of Mirrors. Two hundred fifty acres were used in the construction of the **Gardens of Versailles**, with a mile-long grand canal and 1,400 fountains. Although few of the fountains are still operative, some splendid ones are—you may be lucky enough to see Apollo standing in his chariot, driving four horses through the jetting water, to the salutes of half-immersed tritons. The fountains are operated every Sunday from 3:30 to 5:00 pm from May to September. Tickets to the palace and grounds are 30F ($6), but only 15F ($3) on Sunday. Phone: 39-50-36-22.

The **Grand and Petit Trianons** are not included in Versailles' general admission charge. They are closed on Mondays and holidays, but are open from 9:45 am to noon and 2:00 to 5:30 pm on other days. Admission is 13F for the Grand Trianon and 8F for the Petit Trianon, which also admits you to the coach museum containing ornate carriages from the 18th and 19th centuries. Just past the Trianons lies **Le Hameau**, Marie Antoinette's playtime sheep ranch.

Fireworks and illuminated fountains are offered several times a year, usually on Saturday nights. Bleacher seats are for sale at the tourist office in Versailles, located at 7, rue des Réservoirs. Prices range from 80 to 180F ($16-36), depending upon where you sit.

Hotels

If you are planning to spend Saturday night at Versailles, it is advisable to make advance reservations. A call from a Paris phone is not expensive and could save you much grief. All of these hotels are near the palace.

The **Bellevue Hotel** (12, ave. de Sceaux) is recently remodeled. Rates: 450F ($90), with parking 12F ($2.50). Phone: 39-50-13-41.

La Résidence du Berry (14, rue Anjou) was totally updated in 1987. Rates: 370-440F ($74-88), with free parking. Phone: 39-49-07-07.

Hôtel Richaud (16, rue Richaud) is farthest from the palace, but still an easy walk. Rates: 280-350F ($56-70), with free parking. Phone: 39-50-10-42.

Restaurants

The tearoom at the **Palais Trianon** hotel (1, blvd. de la Reine) is worth the price of 65F ($13) for a "high tea." Dress your best (men in jackets and neckties) and eat all you can hold from the trays of *patisseries*. Phone: 30-84-38-00.

The setting of **La Boule d'Or** (25, rue du Maréchal Foch) makes you feel as though you have been transported back to the 17th century. Menus: 200-300F ($40-60), with wine extra. Phone: 39-50-22-97.

A less expensive choice would be the country-style inn **Le Dauphin** (24-26, Grande-Rue). Here the menu starts at 150F ($30). Closed on Tuesdays and Wednesdays and all of February. Phone: 64-22-27-04.

Chartres

The magnificent cathedral dominates the town, and many visitors see little beyond it. An extra day here can provide a welcome rest from busy Paris.

Attractions

The **Vieux Quartier** (Old Town) radiates from the cathedral, each street lined with ancient dwellings, some of which date back to the 12th century. The facades are often colorful, and the bridges across the River Eure are very picturesque—all in all, a photographer's dream setting.

The **Musée des Beaux-Arts** (29, Cloître Notre-Dame) is located near the cathedral and contains not only the expected works of 16th- to 19th-century artists, e.g. Brosamer and Watteau, but also a large collection of works by the post-impressionist Maurice de Vlaminck. Phone: 37-36-41-39.

Hotels

Le Grand Monarque (22, place des Epars), a member of Best Western International, is built around a lovely courtyard which provides a peaceful view from the comfortable rooms. It's expensive, but full of old-world charm. Rates: 460-705F ($92-141). Phone: 37-21-00-72.

Hotel de la Poste (3, rue du Général-Koenig) is a member of the Logis de France, which says much for its cleanliness and comfort. Soundproof walls and wall-to-wall carpet may make you think you're at home. Rates: 205-280F ($41-60). Phone: 37-21-04-27.

Restaurants

Le Grand Monarque (22, place des Epars) restaurant in the hotel has a fine menu starting at 200F ($40), and the setting is as grand as the name suggests. Phone: 37-21-00-72.

Henri IV (31, rue Soleil d'Or) rates a star from Michelin and has one of the most extensive wine cellars in France. Closed July 30-August 22. The menu is not unusually pricey, starting at 250F ($50), but it is easy to get carried away by the wine list. Phone: 37-36-01-56.

La Vieille Maison (5, rue au Lait) is located across from the cathedral in an ancient building. Fresh fish is a specialty here. Closed Sundays and Mondays. Menus: 220-340F ($45-65). Phone: 37-34-10-07.

Olivet-Orléans

Olivet lies a mere five miles south of Orléans along the banks of the Loire River. The town has little to offer the tourist beyond the enormous park and rose gardens built around Le Source (details in Chapter 3), but the historic city of Orléans is worth a stop. Or, if you find a hotel that is particularly pleasing, Orléans offers a central place from which to visit the numerous châteaux in the Loire valley. However, the city of Tours would be a better home base if visiting the châteaux is your primary goal.

Attractions

As would be expected, references to Jeanne d'Arc are ubiquitous at the site of her greatest triumph, pervading even the **Cathédrale Saint-Croix**, located at the head of rue Jeanne d'Arc. In the north transept, you will find the altar decorated with a carving of the battle scenes from 1429 and a statue of the Maid of Orléans standing on a pedestal held by two golden leopards representing the defeated English. Phone: 38-66-64-17.

Place du Martroi displays the most-often-photographed equestrian statue of the armored St. Joan. This square is the heart of the old city, but there are few old buildings which survived the aerial bombings of World War II.

The **Groslot Hôtel** on the place de l'Etap, between the cathedral and place du Martoi, dates from 1550. Francis II died there in December 1560, leaving his widow, Mary Queen of Scots, to face her destiny at the hands of Queen Elizabeth I. The statue of Joan of Arc, praying at the foot of the stairs, was done by Princess Marie, daughter of King Louis Philippe. Phone: 38-42-22-30.

Hotels

Le Rivage (635, rue Reine-Blanche) is the hotel in Olivet we were originally hoping to find. (We missed the turn-off at the first left after crossing the bridge from Orléans.) This is a small, quiet hotel with views of the river and a good restaurant. Closed in February. Rates: 350-450F ($70-90). Phone: 38-66-02-93.

St-Martin (52, blvd. Alexandre-Martin) is near the cathedral and other sights, but only half of the rooms have showers or tubs. Be sure to ask. Rates: 266F ($53) with bath. Phone: 38-62-47-47.

Terminus (40, rue de la République) is located across the street from the train station, but all rooms have bath or shower facilities. Remodeled in 1990, the rooms are quiet and comfortable. Parking is an extra 40F ($8). Rates: 325-370F ($65-74). Phone: 38-53-24-64.

Restaurants

The restaurant at **Le Rivage** is excellent, and if you are fortunate enough to get a room in the hotel, by all means have dinner here. Menus: 160-270F ($32-54).

Les Antiquaires (2-4, rue au Lin) features an air-conditioned dining room in a charming old house with exposed ceiling beams. The food is typically French, adjusted for the seasonal availability of such things as fresh salmon from the Loire. Local wines are both cheap and good— try a red Chinon or a white Sancerre. Closed August 1 through August 24. Menus: 190-290F ($38-58). Phone: 38-53-52-35.

La Grange (205, faubourg Bourgogne, route de Nevers, St-Jean-de-Braye) is a couple of miles east of Orléans on highway N152. The building is an old converted barn, but the kitchen is thoroughly modern. Closed the entire month of August. Menus: 100-140F ($20-28). Phone: 38-86-43-36.

Along the rue de Bourgogne, parallel to the Loire River, you will find a number of small restaurants, each featuring the cuisine of a particular ethnic group. For example, the **Crêperie Breton** (#242) will provide a satisfying meal for less than 75F ($15), and **Le Madras** (#152) has an Indian menu at 48F ($10). There are many others.

Chapter 3

From the Ridiculous to the Sublime: Clermont-Ferrand & Brioude

We awoke with unhappy memories from the preceding night's disastrous dinner and were reluctant to again trust our digestive systems to the inept hands of the hotel staff. However, convenience triumphed over experience, and with a certain trepidation, we again entered the restaurant. *Incroyable! Le petit déjeuner* was simple and efficiently served. The waitress recorded our room number, then brought wonderfully rich, black coffee and a pitcher of steaming hot milk while we made our selection of fruit and rolls from the buffet table.

As we checked out, a brochure at the desk caught my eye. Le Source, it advised, was a sight not to miss. A branch of the Loire River went underground several kilometers to the south, to reappear in the form of an artesian well in Olivet. An extensive park had been built around the resurgent waters, with massive plantings of tulips and daffodils for the spring and large beds of roses for the summer visitors. "We should see this," I said to Wendy. "It's on our way."

"On our way?" She questioned, "Where are we going?"

"South," I answered, quick to allay any suspicion that I had not the foggiest idea of what our next destination would be. "When we get to the park, I'll open Old Gray and show you on the map."

She gave me her I-can-see-right-through-you look. "Okay, you're the driver. On to the park."

The park exceeded its billing. Meticulously planted beds of flowers lay on either side of a vast stretch of green lawn, and a small stream meandered down the center. The pathway led from one planting to another, crossing the stream on miniature oriental bridges. A scattering of trees served to break the visual plane at strategic spots, framing flower beds so that each could be fully appreciated without interference from the next. Marigolds, yellow and orange of varying heights, were accented by the marine blue of lobelia borders. The beds on either side of the entrance were planted with ornamental cabbages, set in precise, geometric designs as intricate as a Persian rug, with colors of red, purple, and creamy white, the whole making a gorgeous paisley print of living vegetables.

A small, rubber-tired train was available for the sedentary and infirm, but it was such a beautiful morning that we elected to walk; besides, most of the cars were filled with boisterous children. We slowly sauntered down the path, feeling like a couple from Georges Seurat's "Sunday in the Park" painting, as we marveled at the mass plantings.

After we left the flower beds, the trees became more numerous, creeping onto the grassy field like the vanguard of a forest. The distant sounds of the children on their train could no longer be heard. But in the near-silence, the faint sound of bubbling water came from somewhere ahead, and we hurried toward it. Another turn around a rocky outcropping and there it was. Not a tall column of sparkling clear water, surging up like a geyser, just a gentle trickle of water overflowing a pool situated in a rocky grotto. We had come to Le Source.

Back in the car, we pulled the maps out of Old Gray and determined the course for the next stage of our adventure. The town of Clermont-Ferrand, located in the mountainous terrain of the Massif Central, was within an easy day's drive, and the name conjured up a vision of a quaint village nestled in a river valley with a sweeping view of the surrounding mountains.

With windows cranked down, for the day was becoming warm, we pressed southward, entering and leaving roundabout after roundabout, resisting the temptation of a side trip to Tours or Blois in the Loire Valley. Each traffic circle brought a fresh reminder of the French propensity for tailgating a bewildered traveler. The rule is: those already in a roundabout have the right of way. Loosely translated, this means: enter at your peril. Those drivers behind me always seemed eager to hazard the fray and, if I hesitated for a second, would bring their car's howling engine to within feet of our vulnerable rear, increasing the anxiety. Once the proper exit was spotted, leaving the roundabout was simply a matter of swinging around the circle until a clear path was assured. Simple, unless some madman rides your rear bumper like a hog after truffles. I have been known to make as many as three complete circles before being released. I envied those French drivers, so sure of their skill, so certain of their reflexes.

After one particularly harrowing merry-go-round ride, Wendy remarked, "Now we know why the French are so strict about wearing seat belts."

"What they need is a restraining belt for the driver's right foot," I replied.

But now we were free of the congested roads leading to the Loire Valley; the last roundabout was behind us, and the road stretched ahead in a gradual slope to the Massif Central. We slipped through the town of Châteauroux, then shifted down as the road assumed a steeper slope.

As we climbed ever higher, the first of the area's castles thrust its shattered battlements above a jutting crag, a ruined monument to the futility of war. I pulled off the road for a better view, welcoming the chance to detach my mind from the mundane task of driving and giving it free rein to wander back through the centuries to the time of the Hundred Years War. In my imagination, I could see the castle walls whole, banners flowing from the turrets, and armored knights on horseback, their bright shields flashing in the sun. For a hundred years, four generations, those walls stood, promising safety to the poor peasants who worked the land and prayed on Sundays for a better kingdom yet to come.

"I'm hungry." Wendy's voice interrupted my reverie.

A glance at my watch revealed that noon had already slipped by us. "Want to go back to Châteauroux?" I asked. "I'm not sure there's a town big enough to have a restaurant within miles of us ahead."

"Never go back," Wendy said. "We'll find something."

A few miles up the road, I pulled off at a rest stop filled with parked cars. "Why are we stopping here?" Wendy asked.

I pointed to a bright aluminum van with a hand-printed sign on top bearing the single word "frites." "Lunch," I replied. "Find a spot, and I'll bring the food."

As I studied the simple menu printed on a blackboard behind the counterman, I casually withdrew my wallet. Two hot dogs would be twenty francs and two beers would add another twenty. A small dish of *frites* was fifteen francs, bringing the total to fifty-five. I glanced in my wallet to discover only a single fifty-franc note. I felt in my pockets for coins, but could come up with only one twenty-centime piece, one franc and one half-franc, a total of 1.7 francs. In a city, credit cards can be used almost everywhere, and cash is easily obtainable at ATMs, but this was the country. Sheepishly, I beat a hasty retreat.

Wendy had found a nice spot for a picnic: a patch of grass, an empty bench, and a sweeping view of the valley below. She looked up as I approached. "Where's the food?"

"Do you have any money?"

She reached deep within her purse. "Only this," she said, and held out a ten-franc coin. Its silver center gleamed within the encircling brass. At the moment, it seemed the most beautiful coin in the world.

This time I returned with food in hand, and we settled down to serious eating. A cooling breeze moved through the trees, stirring the leaves in a gentle dance. We were utterly content, munching the mustardy hot dogs, drinking the beer out of the cans, and dropping the *frites* into our mouths one at a time, like a Hollander eating herring. "That was the last of the *frites*," Wendy teased as I lifted the strip of fried potato to my lips.

"We had better get moving if we're going to make Clermont today," I said, thinking as much about finding an ATM to replenish our cash as of a hotel for the night. My face must have reflected my inner concern.

"Remember," Wendy cautioned as we started up, "this is supposed to be a fun trip."

For the most part, the road followed the crest of a ridge overlooking the small tributary streams that converged behind us to form the Loire River. Country roads in France will often follow the ridges of the hills, rather than the valley floors as they do in the United States. The thrifty French long ago seem to have decided that fertile valley land was too valuable to waste on roads. Heavy clumps of scrub pine and oak edged our path, but every mile or so the vegetation opened, and we were treated to sudden panoramic views down into the valleys, where all was lush and green. Occasionally, we would see the remnants of yet another castle clinging forlornly to some rocky crest.

The traffic picked up perceptibly as we made the descent into Clermont-Ferrand. Where we had been expecting a quaint mountain village, we found instead a bustling center of commerce. It was only later that we discovered that Clermont-Ferrand was the headquarters of the Michelin empire. Trucks and cars filled every street, and stoplights required attention at every corner. It was four o'clock, the height of the rush hour, and our time to stop. "Maybe we can find a Novotel or an Ibis," I said, trying to mask my vexation at being faced with a second night of standardized mediocrity at a chain motel.

"I'd even settle for a Mercure," Wendy replied, naming the most luxurious of the chains. "Let's just get out of this."

"Maybe we'll find something at the other end of town," I replied through clenched teeth, as I hurriedly braked to avoid a car that suddenly changed lanes, cutting in ahead of us. I instinctively braced myself for a rear-end collision from the truck that had been pressing us from behind. Apparently the driver had seen what was happening and had reacted in time to stop with a full six inches to spare.

"Like good old L.A.!" Wendy exclaimed.

The twenty minutes or so that it took to traverse the town seemed an eternity, and I could feel the nervous perspiration gathering in soppy patches on my back long before the traffic began to thin and patches of open fields replaced factory buildings and warehouses.

"Novotel, two kilometers," Wendy exclaimed triumphantly, pointing to a sign. "And Ibis, but I didn't catch how far." I slowed as much as the traffic would allow, alert now for the next sign, having resigned myself to the inevitable. The large, two-story Novotel loomed ahead.

We turned into the drive with mixed feelings. It was a relief to be out of the traffic, and we would have a clean, comfortable bed for the night, but the thought of facing another of those generic, quick-fix restaurants brought on a sense of defeat. After all, one did not travel all the way to France to eat at Denny's.

The clerk looked up from his newspaper and muttered, "*Complet.*"

"*Complet*? Full?" I asked incredulously.

"*Oui, monsieur. Je suis désolé.*"

I thought, not half as *désolé* as I am. I tried to retrieve the French words to ask where Ibis would find itself, but all I could muster was a feeble, "*L'hôtel Ibis? C'est près d'ici?*"

"*A gauche.*" The man swung his left hand clutching the newspaper and added, "*C'est en face de la rue.*"

"*Merci,*" I replied and beat a hasty retreat to the car to confer with Wendy.

"No room. They're filled up. And he says Ibis is back toward town, facing the road, but I sure didn't see it."

"Back toward town!" Now Wendy looked désolée. "Let's just go on. We'll find something better."

"The next town of any size is Le Puy," I said, studying the map. "Should be about an hour's drive."

"Le Puy," Wendy savored the name. "Poohwee. I wonder what it means."

"The dictionary's in Old Gray. We'll have to check it later, after we find a place to stop."

With that happy thought, we took the road that climbed out of the valley of Clermont-Ferrand and headed south across the scrub and granite of the Massif Central. We were in the high plateau country that collected the winter snows and filtered the spring runoff through a hundred lakes to form the headwaters of the Cher and Loire Rivers to the north and the Dordogne to the west. Mile by mile, with each turning of the road, the vegetation gradually changed from scrub oak to pine to chestnut to open grassland dotted with flocks of sheep.

An hour had passed since leaving Clermont-Ferrand, and Wendy anxiously studied the signs at each town and small village along the way. Issoire looked too commercial to warrant a stop, and Saint Germain-Lembron seemed too small to offer accommodations for the night.

One sign beside a wide, ornate gate caught her attention: "Le Château de Louis XV." Louis XV was the forgotten king of France, his reign sandwiched between the time of the Sun King, Louis XIV, and that of the husband to Marie Antoinette, Louis XVI.

"Let's look," Wendy said, and we turned in at the chestnut-arched drive. The château looked very much like an oversized, stone farm house except for the massive chimneys which were decorated with the royal crest. The walls and the shelter over the carriage entrance were covered with tangles of still-blooming wisteria. In place of the cobblestones which might have been expected, the courtyard was covered with loose gravel, which crunched beneath our feet as we walked to the entrance.

Admission was ten francs apiece. I reached for my wallet and suddenly remembered. We had spent the last of our money on hot dogs. I offered the Visa card to the lady at the ticket booth, feeling like Oliver Twist asking for more gruel.

"*Non,*" she said firmly, "*nous n'acceptons pas la carte bleue.*"

"Maybe we can come back." Wendy tried to sound hopeful.

"Probably nothing there but old furniture," I said, adding a dose of sour grapes to assuage my guilt about the cash deficit. I had planned to replenish our supply of pocket money in Clermont, but had forgotten all about it. "Anyway, we still have to find a place to stay tonight. Let's go."

Back on the road, the shadows had lengthened, and the sun would momentarily disappear behind the taller peaks that lined the valley of the Allier River. We passed more small towns and villages, but it became difficult in the fading light to make out their names. Directional signs continued to indicate that Le Puy was just ahead, but where? Finally, we entered an area with larger houses, gardens planted along the road, stop lights at the corners, and real stores with sidewalks. We had arrived. "Look for a hotel sign," I urged, knowing that Wendy had already begun her search.

"There," she said, "L'hôtel de la Poste."

I pulled over for a closer look. The facade looked rather drab under its coating of road dust accumulated during the summer, and the suspicious looks from the men sipping beer at tables in front of a small café alongside the entrance were not promising. Our arrival, in a car bearing Paris license plates, seemed to be a matter of considerable concern.

"They probably think we're from the government, here to help them," Wendy surmised. However, a glimpse into the lobby was reassuring; it was bright and looked clean and well-kept. Besides, it was getting late, and our options were becoming fewer by the minute.

I got out of the car. "Wait here. I'll check."

Wendy cast a glance at the men on the sidewalk and said, "I'll go with you."

All doubts vanished as we entered the spotless lobby, decorated with walnut furnishings on oriental rugs, the walls covered with a pale golden wallpaper that would say "French" in any country. Baskets of green ferns were used to accent the corners of the room, and on the desk, an enormous bouquet of hydrangeas proclaimed the attentive care of a staff that prided itself on its work. We were greeted by a young woman who answered my inquiry with a pleasant smile and a "yes."

"*Désirez-vous une chambre tranquille?*" she asked.

Delighted at the prospect, I completely forgot to use French and replied, "You bet!"

She looked puzzled for a moment before asking, "*Américain?*"

"*Oui,*" Wendy and I said in unison.

"You wait," she said in careful English, "I will get my husband."

"I think we blew it!" Wendy said, but before I could reply "You bet," the young woman returned with her husband.

"Your car?" he questioned.

I pointed out the door, and he said, "You follow me."

"In the car?"

He nodded his head in agreement and walked out to a little white pickup truck. "You follow me," he repeated.

"If the place looks bad, we won't even get out of the car," I assured Wendy as we started out, following the truck up a hill, around a stone-walled truck farm, across a field and then back downhill through a gate and into the courtyard of an enormous ranch-style home. The truck was parked at the door, with the young man standing beside it. He indicated with a sweep of his arm that we should park under some trees at the far end of the paved surface of the driveway. Walking from the car, we could look out over the town in the valley below, with the last rays of the sun putting a rusty glow on the roof tiles.

"This is my parents' . . . no, this is my parents' of my wife's house." The young man's struggle with English was obviously as painful as my struggles with French. He opened the door into a large entrance hall. "They live there." He pointed toward a set of double doors that led off to the left of the hall. "Your room is here." He unlocked a door to the right, revealing a beautifully appointed room, complete with a TV set and modern bathroom with shower.

"It's lovely." Wendy said, sinking onto the bed.

The young man put the keys on the TV and asked, "*Dîner?*"

Suddenly, I was very hungry. "Of course," I answered.

"Come." He led the way back out to the courtyard, around the corner of the house onto the terraced lawn. He pointed to the lower end of the walled property. "Gate is there. *L'hôtel* is there." He raised his finger and, sure enough, there was the hotel, not more than two blocks away. We had looped around in following the road, to end just about where we had started.

It took but a moment to freshen up and walk down the hill. The dining room occupied the entire second story of the hotel. Its walls were of polished wood, set off with large brass-framed mirrors which warmly reflected the light from the brass chandeliers. The tables were set with lace covers and crisp white napkins, and on each was a small vase of fresh-cut carnations. We were seated and given a choice from three menus, varying mainly in the number of courses. We chose the middle ground, which included soup, hors d'oeuvres, salad, entrée, cheese and dessert. The wine list offered something for every taste and price range desired.

The soup was a marvelous combination of summer vegetables which had been simmered for hours in a chicken stock. The stock did not intrude, but rather served as a delicate balance, as the flavors merged, until all was blended into a single, yet amazingly complex flavor. We had finished off the basket of fresh-baked bread and had second helpings of the soup before Wendy called a cautionary halt. "This is just the first course!"

I could have made a meal on only the soup and bread, but if the rest of the courses were as good, I knew that I would be sorry for not having saved room. Reluctantly, I put the ladle back in the tureen.

As we progressed through the meal, we determined through fractured French and English on both sides that the hotel was a family venture. Madame, a regal lady in a dress of flowered silk, was hostess and order taker, while monsieur served as waiter and busboy. One daughter, whom we had first met, acted as receptionist, and the second daughter did the cooking. The son-in-law performed the duties of general handyman.

We had each ordered *coquelet au vin à l'ancienne* for our entrées, and as soon as we caught the aroma rising from the plates, we knew that this was no pen-raised, gruel-fed fowl. This was a full-fledged rooster. Cut off in his prime, he had been simmered with white wine, small onions, wild mushrooms, and savory herbs known only to the chef. A generous dollop of sweet, fresh cream, added at the last moment, blended the flavors into a sublime, soul-satisfying gravy.

After we had cleaned our plates of the marvelous chicken, Madame stopped by to see if everything was to our liking. After assuring her of our culinary rapture, and not being sure of the pronunciation of "Le Puy," we asked her guidance. *"Que diton en français le nom de cette ville?"* I asked. She responded, *"Brioude."* I thought she was helping me to pronounce the name of the Beaujolais from the Bruilly district which we were drinking.

"Non," I responded and, taking a pen in hand, wrote the name "Le Puy" on a bit of paper. *"Que dit on le nom de cette ville."* Faced with such garbled language, it was a wonder that Madame

could contain her composure, but she smiled in a grandmotherly fashion and slowly pronounced *"Poohee."* Wendy shot me a look of triumph.

Along with the cheese plate, Monsieur brought a little pamphlet advertising the hotel. On the back, a map showed exactly how to reach it. A large red arrow led from the name "Hotel de la Poste et Champanne" directly to the town of Brioude, located south of Issoire, but still sixty-one kilometers north of Le Puy. I munched on a bit of Cantal, savoring the way its sharp flavor complemented the last of the wine, as I considered our situation. We were strangers in a strange land, with no money, who did not even know where they were; yet we had been lodged in a beautiful private room and fed like royalty. Some situation!

~ On Your Own ~

Clermont-Ferrand

Clermont-Ferrand was not always a bustling, industrial city. Much remains of the quiet mountain village which pre-dates the arrival of Mademoiselle Daubrée, a niece of Charles Macintosh, who married and subsequently began making rubber balls for the amusement of her children. Thus began the Michelin dynasty and industrialization of the town in 1832.

Attractions

The present city, with its hyphenated name, is the result of the combination of two villages, Clermont and Montferrand, in 1631. The recent restoration of the old Montferrand area provides a glimpse of what life must have been like in the 17th century when the gentry lived in these elegant houses. Follow rue des Jacobins, which begins at the place Delille, the same spot from which Pope Urban II called for the First Crusade in 1095. Immediately behind the place Delille is the Romanesque **Basilique Notre-Dame-du-Port** where, for a franc, you can briefly turn on the interior lights to reveal the delicate carvings on the pillars. Knights and biblical figures are interspersed with vegetation, demonstrating the catholic tastes of the carvers. Over the south portal you can see a stiffly upright Madonna and dwarf-like Child. Phone: 73-91-32-94.

The Gothic **Cathédrale Notre-Dame** is only a couple of blocks from the basilica, but generations apart in style, although it was built only a century later in 1248. Built of dark-gray volcanic stone which the tools of earlier times had been unable to cut, the facade has survived centuries of weather much better than the interior has survived the ravages of man. (All of the interior fixtures were destroyed during the revolution and replaced with clumsy 19th-century work.) Inside, one has the curious feeling that the cathedral at Amiens had been painted black and transported here. Phone: 73-92-46-61.

The **Musée Ranquet** lies behind the cathedral. The museum features a historical display of the area from Roman times onward. Open May-September 10:00 am-noon and 2:00-6:00 pm, closing at 5:00 pm during the remainder of the year. Closed on Sundays and Mondays. Free admission. Phone: 73-37-38-63.

Royat lies a couple of miles to the west of Clermont on road D68 which you can pick up from place de la Victoire next to the cathedral. Popular as a spa in the 19th century and earlier, as evidenced by the ruins of Roman baths in the park, it has lapsed into a comfortable suburb to Clermont. An energetic climb will put you atop one of the nearby *puys* (dead volcanos) for a wonderful view of the surrounding city.

Puy-de-Dôme is about eight miles beyond Royat, also on D68. Its 4,800-foot peak provides a sweeping view of the entire area, and on a clear day you can see Mont Blanc in the Alps. You don't have to climb this one; buses run from the base to the peak for 18F ($3.50) round-trip.

Hotels

Gallieni (51, rue Bonnabaud) is modern, all rooms with bath, and the restaurant is quite good. Rates: 300F ($60), with parking 30F ($6). Phone: 73-93-59-69.

Colbert (19, rue Colbert) is not as new as Gallieni, but it is very comfortable. Rates: 200-280F ($40-56). Phone: 73-93-25-66.

Bordeaux (39, ave. Franklin Roosevelt) is further out of town and without a restaurant. Rates: 185-270F ($37-54). Phone: 73-37-32-32.

Restaurants

Le Clavé (10-12, rue St-Adjutor) has modern decor set in an old stone house, but the menu is classic French. Menus: 150-370F ($30-74). Phone: 73-36-46-30.

La Truffe d'Argent (17, rue Lamartine), right off the main square in town, puts out good food at reasonable prices. Menus: 100-200F ($25-40). Phone: 73-93-22-42.

Le Stromboli (18, rue du Cheval-Blanc) is the place to go for a change from French cuisine—this is a pizza and pasta parlor. Cheap!

Brioude

Little mentioned in guidebooks, Brioude offers a central point, the junction of highway N102 and the Allier River, from which many interesting areas are within easy driving distance. La Chaise-Dieu within the Parc du Livradois-Forez lies to the east, Le Puy to the southeast, and the gorges of the Allier River to the south.

Attractions

Brioude boasts the largest Romanesque church in the Auvergne, **St.-Julienne de Brioude.** A new roof of glazed tiles put on in the 19th century gives it a somewhat oriental look. Within, a warm harmonious feeling is created by the colors of the walls, varying from red through brown to gray. The structure has five chapels, radiating from a central apse, and the nave sports some unusual frescoes showing the tortures of hell being performed by red and green devils.

Villages of the Allier gorge can easily be reached by turning onto the road D585 at Vieille Brioude. You will be particularly entranced with **St.-Ilpize** which perches on a point above the river and is linked to **Villeneuve-d'Allier** on the opposite bank by the frailest of suspension bridges. Further along, a stone bridge unites the two banks at **Lavoûte-Chilhac,** a great place to look at ruins while you enjoy a picnic lunch.

The **Allier** once produced some of the finest salmon fishing in France, although few are caught there now. Trout fishing is still excellent, and a small dam has created a lake for water sports. Check with the tourist office, just south of the town center on highway N102, for regulations on fishing. The campground is always filled during the summer months.

Chavaniac-Lafayette used to be just "Chavaniac" until they added the "Lafayette" in honor of the Marquis who came to the aid of Washington and the American Revolution. The château where the Marquis was born has been restored and maintained in perfect condition by the American Lafayette Memorial Association.

Hotels

Hotel de la Poste et Champanne is the small hotel with a modern annex and fine restaurant at which we stayed. Rates: 130-230F ($26-46). Menus: 65-160F ($13-32). Phone: 71-50-14-62.

La Brivas (a couple of miles south of Brioude on the road to Le Puy—N102) is a good hotel with all the amenities. Closed from November 21 through December. Rates: 210-290F ($42-58). Menus: 90-300F ($18-60). Phone: 71-50-10-49.

Restaurants

There are no restaurants of note locally outside of hotels. In addition to the two above, you might try the one at the **Hôtel Moderne** (12, ave. Victor-Hugo, just off highway N102 from Clermont). Menus: 80-210F ($16-42). Phone: 71-50-07-30.

Chapter 4

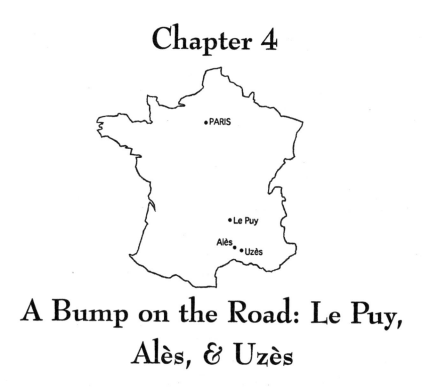

A Bump on the Road: Le Puy, Alès, & Uzès

The next morning, I settled our bill with the plastic card that had been so unceremoniously rejected at Louis XV's place. As I signed the strip of paper, pledging the payment of 563 francs, I felt a smug twinge of pity for our friends at home who had exclaimed, "France? But it's so expensive!" The night's lodging for two in the lovely room with private bath, the sumptuous dinner including the bottle of Brouilly, and the breakfast of *café au lait* with fruit, cheese, and rolls, totaled only $115. That was less than our hotel in Paris without food. Now this, I thought, is the real France.

The temptation was strong to stay another night, but we were committed to visiting both Vence and Albi, so I joined Wendy in the car. She had the map unfolded and, pointing with her finger, said, "See, this is where we are, and this is Le Puy." The two towns were about a finger's width apart on the map. "Do you realize that we came within an inch of missing Brioude entirely?"

"Just be thankful that there was no room at the inn in Clermont," I said, setting the car in motion toward Le Puy.

We arrived at Le Puy about nine in the morning and set out at once to explore the narrow, cobbled streets of the fascinating town. Situated on the ancient, volcanic crest of the Massif Central, the area is dotted with the relics of past geological activity. Unlike the mountainous domes seen in other parts of the world, these were tall, ungainly spires that looked like gigantic versions of African termite nests—the *puys* for which the town was named.

On one particularly large peak that rose several hundred feet into the air, the enterprising people of the Middle Ages had carved out a spiral staircase leading to the top where they built a chapel. We looked at that stairway in awe, trying to imagine the energy that must have been expended on the construction of that chapel. Each stone had to be carried step by aching step, finally to be fitted into the wall rising above the top. Where in the world today could one find such devotion, such total commitment to a faith that required a chapel to be built as close to heaven as possible? We looked at the steep stairway and decided that, even without the need to carry stones, we would not make that climb.

We parked the car, knowing it would be easy to find near that imposing monument, and walked toward the center of town. We passed another of the weird, upthrusting *puys*, this one topped by a misshapen statue which made it look as if there were a cast-iron gargoyle nesting atop the peak. We decided against a closer look, turned and walked along a busy street that promised to lead into the main part of town.

The aroma of fresh-baked pastries from a crowded *pâtisserie* brought a painful reminder that we were out of money. The subliminal desire for a coffee and fresh croissant made it imperative that we find a bank before any further sightseeing. As though in answer to a prayer, there at the next intersection was a Banque Agricole. It took but a moment to insert a card into the ATM, punch in the PIN number, and receive 700 francs in quick cash, but in that moment Wendy had disappeared. It was one thing to be in a foreign country without money, but quite another to lose your wife! Before anxiety turned to panic, Wendy stepped out of a nearby shop.

"Did you get any money?" she asked. "I need to go to a hairdresser. All that heat and dust—my hair's a mess. They said that they can take me right away." She did some mental calculations. "Pick me up in an hour."

An hour. What could I do in an hour? I thought about retracing my steps to the *pâtisserie*, but the lure of the unknown was stronger. Besides, there would probably be another *pâtisserie* somewhere along the way. With that happy thought, I headed on down the street until I came to a large square, teeming with people.

On the plaza and steps of a cathedral, I happened upon the local flea market. Stalls of new and used clothing filled the plaza, while the steps seemed to be reserved for the display of oriental rugs and antique furniture. At one spot, portraits of someone's ancestors peered out of battered frames; at another, a collection of old farm tools was for sale. Everywhere, people were looking, touching, and arguing about quality or price. Nothing there looked fit to eat, so I meandered on through a narrow passage into an adjoining square.

Now here was something to eat: I had discovered the farmers' market. Baskets of freshly picked peaches and nectarines shared a table with boxes of red and green and black grapes, while the next table was laden with boxes of onions, leeks, garlic, and stubby little purple eggplants. Long green beans and tomatoes of varying shapes and sizes were displayed at the next table and flat baskets of crinkly mushrooms were featured at a table next to the cheeses. At that table, a large wheel of blue-veined, creamy looking cheese took center stage beneath the veil of netting in place to discourage flies. Surrounding it were piles of small, gray cylinders that I recognized as goat cheese. And then came the potatoes. Big boxes of baking-sized russets were flanked by smaller boxes of varieties unknown outside the Auvergne. There were small, smooth red potatoes, round white potatoes, and one box of elongated, slender tubers, hardly larger than a man's thumb.

All this produce was but a sideshow compared to the main event at the other end of the square. There, I saw cage after cage of various types of poultry. Chickens of every make and model, from banty hens to the classic French chanticleer, were ready to be sold to enhance someone's farm stock or dinner table. Guinea fowl complained loudly alongside stoic ducks and a large goose, which let out an occasional, nasal squawk.

Farther along were boxes and a few cages filled with rabbits, some as large as Belgian hares, some spotted like Holstein cows, and others, pure white with pink eyes. My favorites were the small, silky, brown bunnies, about the size of the American cottontail. They were allowed to climb from one packing box into another in order to keep track of their friends. Just the sort of animal a boy would wish to have follow him home, even if he knew his mother wouldn't let him keep it. I was so fascinated that I neglected to mind the time. When I did look at my watch, I found that well over a full hour had elapsed since I left Wendy. Happily, I arrived at the beauty shop just as Wendy came out.

"Sorry to keep you waiting," she apologized. "It took a little longer than I thought."

"I allowed for that," I said in a forgiving tone. "Now, come see what I've found." We retraced my steps back to the markets, only to see that the farmers were packing things away. It was noon and the market day was finished. Only a few lop-eared rabbits remained; the cunning little brown fellows had vanished. Providence had again intervened, for I knew that had Wendy seen those animals, she would never again eat rabbit.

The road from Le Puy to Alès descends from the mountainous plateau of the Massif Central to the foothills of Haute Languedoc, passing through several ancient villages as it follows the course of the River Gard. We had stopped for lunch at a roadside *auberge* in Villetor when I noticed that our gas gauge was showing less than a quarter full. Somehow, when renting a car, one feels that everything is taken care of, including an everlasting supply of fuel. An awareness of my own stupidity for not checking when we left Le Puy added to the sense of exasperation and anxiety. It seemed unlikely that we would find a service station before we reached Alès, still miles away. As we passed through the beautiful country, Wendy exclaimed enthusiastically over each castle, each waterfall, each vineyard as we drove by, but my attention was constantly drawn to that harbinger of disaster, the gas gauge.

The countryside began to take on a different look. The vineyards were becoming more extensive, and sunflowers now spread from the road to the crests of gently sloping hills, unlike the small patches we had seen at the higher elevations. The air was noticeably warmer, and more cars had joined us as we approached Alès. The fuel gauge was now registering near empty. "Keep your eyes open for a gas station," I said, pointing to the gauge.

"Good," Wendy replied. "I was wondering if I could hold out until we found a hotel."

The tall Lombardy poplars that make French roads so picturesque made their reappearance shortly before we came to the first roundabout we had seen in days. On the far side of the circle, an isolated building displayed a large, blue-and-white sign with the letters "ELF." "Service station," we said in unison. "I never thought I'd be so glad to see an elf," Wendy added, reflecting my thoughts.

We slowed momentarily to let a car in the circle swing past, before entering. I mentally noted the turn-off slot for Alès, but my attention was focused on the service station, trying to make out the words printed on its canvas awning. Just as we reached the turn-off, the words registered: *sans plomb*. I kept the car steady in its circular path.

"You missed the turn," Wendy sighed.

"I know. *Sans plomb*, no plumbing, no restrooms."

"Are you sure?" She looked dubious.

"That's what the sign said. *Sans plomb*." I tried to reassure her. "There'll be another station soon."

"There'd better be," she replied as we turned out of the circle, once again headed for Alès.

A few miles down the road, we came to another roundabout, this time flanked by two stations. Maneuvering was a little more difficult, as this was a junction with a major highway, but we finally made it to the pumps of the green-and-yellow BP station. I coasted past the pump marked *gasoil*, knowing that our car could not run on diesel, and came to a stop beside the one that proclaimed itself "super." "You hit the restroom while I fill her up," I said, but Wendy was already out of the car and on her way. I never did know if she had seen, printed below the "super" designation, the words "sans plomb." Obviously, not a reference to restrooms.

My mind toyed with the riddle while I filled the tank. *Plomb*? Plumber . . . plumbing . . . plumb the depths . . . plumb bob? What was the common factor? Plumb bob . . . Pb, the chemical symbol for lead . . . a plumber used lead to solder pipes. My sense of elation could not have been greater had I been the one to crack the code of the Rosetta stone. My initial assumption had not been too far off, but what a difference in the meaning. *Sans plomb* . . . without lead . . . unleaded!

We reached Alès in the early afternoon and were delighted to see the tourist bureau a few hundred feet beyond the large turn-about at the city's entrance. Tourist bureaus are often helpful, not only in finding hotel rooms, but also in providing information about the town and surrounding country—information not found in the guidebooks. And best of all, there is usually someone that can relay the information in English.

Coming out of the roundabout, my attention was focused on the bureau parking area, and as we made the turn, our car was sent surging into the driveway by a sudden thrust, accompanied by the sounds of shattering glass and the screech of rubber on pavement. I stopped the car, automatically put it in neutral, and turned to look through the rear window.

"She hit us!" Wendy said in shocked disbelief.

"Sure felt like it," I replied and got out of the car to assess the damage. The other car sat forlornly at the entrance to the driveway. Its right fender was crumpled, the headlight ensemble dangling like a broken toy from an assortment of wires. I looked at our car, noting with annoyance that in the confusion I had neglected to shut off the turn signal which was still blinking reproachfully. I looked for signs of damage, but the only evidence of impact was a small dent in the middle of the bumper. Our turn into the driveway had lifted us to a level where the most substantial part of our car had been struck by the most vulnerable part of the other car. I touched the dent and dislodged a bit of brown paint from the other car that had been transferred by the force of the impact.

My attention was soon diverted by sounds of anger and frustration emanating from the driver of the brown car. She was a tall, well-dressed woman of mature age, but her words were as indecipherable as if they came from a child in the throes of a temper tantrum. It was French, but not like any I had heard before. My mind raced, trying to put together the words and phrases I would need. What was the word for hit? *Frappe* came, but I knew that was some sort of ice cream. *Coupe*? No, that was a soup dish. I took a step forward and said, "*Bonjour, madame.*"

She looked at me as though I were mad. "*Bonjour?*" she shrieked and gestured wildly at her car. More words I could not understand began pouring out, accompanied by emphatic pointing, first at her car, then at our car, then at me. The only interpretation I could make of the entire diatribe was that, somehow, the collision must have been my fault. My survival instincts took over. When she paused for breath, I tried the words I had rehearsed in my mind. "*Pourquoi avez-vous me frappé?*"

I guess she understood me, because the question elicited a new stream of French, which I still could not understand, although there was no mistaking the indignation. While I stood absorbing the woman's invective, Wendy had quietly gone to the tourist office, seeking aid. She returned with a young woman who, after listening to the other driver's complaint, said in perfect English, "She says that you did not signal a turn."

In amazement, I turned and gestured toward the still blinking light.

The young woman looked amused. "You have insurance?" she asked and repeated the question in French to the other woman.

"Yes," I answered and hurried to get the packet of papers from the glove compartment. When I returned, the two women were in a weighty discussion.

"I do not do the insurance forms," the tourist agent explained. "That must be done at the insurance office." She looked at the large red packet in my hand and continued, "You are in luck. Their office is just a few kilometers down this street."

She turned toward the other driver and, I assumed, related the same message, because the older woman nodded her head in assent and marched back to her car. "She knows where the office is. If you follow her, you will have no trouble."

"Okay, I'll follow her," I said, "but I'm not getting in front of her again."

She shrugged her shoulders and added, "They can call me if they wish. I'll be here for another hour."

"I can't thank you enough," I said and really meant it. "By the way, what language was she speaking? It sounded like French, but I couldn't understand a word."

"Languedoc," she answered. "The old ones often use it."

The older woman was back in her car, glaring impatiently at me through the window.

"Thanks again for everything," I said as I got in our car.

"Is that it?" Wendy asked. "Can we go now?" She grimaced when I explained that we had to stop at the car rental agency. "She expects us to pay for her car after she hit us? It was her fault, and she expects us to pay?"

"We'll let the rental agency worry about that," I replied. "It shouldn't take long." And it didn't. After listening to the woman's complaint, making a telephone call to the tourist bureau, and an inspection of the two cars, the clerk handed back our papers and waved us on our way with the cheery Americanism, "Have a nice day."

"I don't think I like Alès," Wendy said. "How far is the next town?"

I looked at the map. "About a half-hour to Uzès."

"Let's go for it." Wendy expressed my feelings exactly.

The ancient town of Uzès is built on a high bluff overlooking the valley of the Gard River, not far from the spectacular and often-photographed Pont du Gard. The walls surrounding the inner city were built on foundations laid by the Romans and added to throughout the Middle Ages, when the Popes resided at Avignon. Within this inner wall is the beautifully preserved ducal palace—a feudal castle, complete with battlements, turrets and spires.

We stopped for coffee in view of the castle, while I thumbed through the *Michelin Guide*, looking for a reference to the imposing structure. Our resulting conjecture was interrupted by a French man who informed us that this was still the home of a family that traced its ancestry back to the days of Charlemagne. The sloping roof of a massive tower proudly displayed the family crest on a shield of gold tiles against a background of red, which could be seen from the road approaching the city.

The cathedral was constructed immediately abutting the inner-city walls, on the side that provides a sweeping view of the valley below. Several levels of terrace, planted in orchards and flower gardens, lie below the plaza, which is separated from such worldly undertakings by a marble balustrade. It was this peaceful, panoramic vista that led Jean Racine, the 17th-century French dramatist, to spend a year away from the court at Versailles. A plaque to commemorate his stay in Uzès also serves to mark the vantage point he thought provided the most beautiful view in southern France.

We located the *Bureau du Tourisme*, only to find that all the town's hotel rooms were filled. However, the obliging gentleman in charge made a few phone calls to locate a room for us at a hotel a few kilometers out of town. He even arranged for them to hold a room until we could arrive.

Once there we found our hotel, the St. Géniès, typical of the tourist inns that were abundant before the advent of the motel chains and which can still be found in the smaller towns of rural France. Although it was old, probably having passed through several generations of family ownership, it was well cared for and scrupulously clean. Our room had the usual bidet and shower, but the toilet had been added at some later date and was squeezed into a corner, leaving the user wedged between the basin and wall. In meeting the conflicting demands of privacy and comfort in a limited space, comfort had lost.

The only real drawback to this tranquil hotel was the absence of a restaurant. We would have to drive back into town if we wanted dinner and, of course, we did. Our host telephoned to make reservations for us at the L'Alexandry, not only a fine restaurant in his mind, but one which he thought we could easily find. He was right on both assumptions.

We dined on whole, grilled Dover sole, anointed with butter and dusted with shaved almonds. At first, we were somewhat taken aback by the size of the fish, which more than covered the entire plate, leaving the head and tail sticking over at either side. But one taste convinced us that no serving would be too large. A bottle of chilled Sancerre was a perfect accompaniment to the fish, the salad, and the cheese that followed. Fresh local peaches, picked at the exact time of perfect ripeness, completed the meal. Reluctant to leave, we poured the last of the wine and ordered coffee. The perfect end to a challenging day.

"I've got to admire the way you maintained your calm today," Wendy said. "I was so furious that I could have hit that woman, but you just stood there, cool and collected."

"It wasn't that I was cool and collected, I just didn't know what she was saying. Like that old saying—'if you can keep your head while all about you are losing theirs, you just don't understand the situation.' Well, I sure didn't understand." I squeezed her hand. "You were the one that kept her cool. We might still be in Alès if you hadn't found that tourist lady."

"All in all, an interesting day," she concluded and finished the last of her coffee. "Think you can find the hotel?"

It was dark. It became even darker as we left the lights of Uzès behind. I put the headlights on high beam, but was immediately greeted by the angry flashing of lights from an approaching car. I returned our lights to the low, amber glow that did nothing to illuminate the road, but only served to warn approaching cars of our presence. I slowed, peering vainly into the gloom ahead, alert for any twist or turn in the road. Another car, displaying more confidence than caution, overtook and passed us with a taunting toot of the horn. It seemed an eternity before I recognized the turnoff to the hotel.

Safely in our room, I couldn't help commenting on our travels and travails thus far. "Do you realize that we have already broken just about every rule of our trip?"

"Yeah," Wendy replied, "hasn't it been fun?"

~ On Your Own ~

Le Puy

Le Puy (Le Puy-en-Velay) is enough to warrant a visit at any time; the site alone is given a three-star rating by Michelin.

Attractions

Your pleasure in Le Puy will be doubled if you can time your visit to coincide with the second week in September, when the **Roi de l'Oiseau** (King of the Birds) festival is in full celebration. Costumed in medieval garb, minstrels, jesters, townspeople, and archers rove the streets. The climax comes at the archers' tournament with the crowning of the winning archer.

The **Cathédrale de Notre-Dame**, while Romanesque in style, exhibits a strong influence from Byzantium and North Africa. The building is curiously striped with alternate rows of light and dark stone and, like much of Le Puy, requires considerable climbing to explore. Entrance to the church is free, but if you wish to see the adjoining Cloisters and the Chapel of Relics and Religious Art Treasures, tickets are only 20F ($4). On view are many vestments, gold and silver crosses, enameled cups, etc. Phone: 73-62-11-45.

The **Jardin Henry-Vinay** lies between the bustling place du Breul and the river (actually the headwaters of the Loire) and offers a welcome respite from climbing. The park's **Musée Crozatier** offers a large display of lace along with assorted paintings and carvings dating from the 14th century to the present.

Twenty-five miles north of Le Puy, in the direction of Ambert, lies the small, mountain town of **La Chaise-Dieu** (the chair of God). Only the brooding, medieval abbey church, with its square Norman towers, differentiates this town from a thousand other charming, rustic villages. The interior of the church makes it truly remarkable. Dated from the 15th century—the time of the Black Death, leprosy plague, and the Hundred Years war—an ominously uncompleted fresco depicts the shadowy figure of Death caressing the fat flesh of unaware humans as they cavort about. Near the church, on the place de l'Echo, is the fascinating Salle de l'Echo, used in medieval times as a confession room for the very sick and dying. It was constructed so that two people could sit in opposite corners of the room, with their backs to each other, and still converse in perfectly audible whispers—amazing acoustical science applied to prevent contagion. To reach La Chaise-Dieu, take route N102 north out of Le Puy onto route D906 in the direction of Ambert.

Hotels

Hôtel Chris'tel (15, blvd. Alexandre-Clair), in the newer part of town not far from the Jardin Henry-Vinay, offers comfortable rooms with large windows opening onto a balcony. Breakfast only. Rates: 370-400F ($74-80), with parking 30F ($6). Phone: 71-02-24-44.

The Parc (4, ave. Clément Charbonnier), a little closer to the old town, is also without a restaurant, but has all of the modern amenities. Rates: 350-400F ($70-80), with parking 30F ($6). Phone: 71-02-40-40.

Restaurants

Sarda (12, rue Chênebouterie) offers classic French cuisine along with a variety of regional dishes. An unusual note: unlike in the vast majority of French restaurants, dogs are not permitted in the dining room(!). Closed Sundays and Mondays. Menus: 125-375F ($25-75). Phone: 71-09-58-94.

Le Bâteau Ivre (5, rue Portail-d'Avignon) is decorated in a rustic style, although the cooking is Continental at its best. Closed Sundays and Mondays and the first two weeks in November. Menus: 100-280F ($20-56). Phone: 71-09-67-20.

For a cheaper meal that is very good, try the restaurant at the **Hôtel La Verveine** (place Cadelade). Menus: 80-175F ($16-35). Phone: 71-02-00-77.

Alès

To those weary of cathedrals, ancient ruins, and exhausting museums, Alès offers a brief respite in a modern French community of wide avenues, parks, and comfortable hotels.

Attractions

If you must see something of historical note, the **Cathédrale St.-Jean** boasts an interesting old Romanesque facade with a Gothic porch attached, although the rest of the construction dates from only the 18th century. The **Musée du Colombier** is in a restored château, set in a pretty garden. Inside, the main attraction is a display of wrought iron. Paintings from the 16th to 20th centuries fill two floors.

Hotels

The **Grand Hôtel** (17, bis place Gabriel-Péri) may be old, but it's quite comfortable and within a block of the banks of the River Gard. The restaurant is closed Saturdays and Sundays, and all of December and January. Rates: 250-400F ($50-80). Phone: 66-52-19-01.

Uzès

Its proximity to the famous Roman ruins at Nîmes, the finest example of Roman construction at Pont du Gard, and the town of Arles, where Van Gogh produced his turbulent paintings, has resulted in an unfortunate bypassing of this lovely town by most tourists. With no trace of Roman antiquities, and little from the medieval, the feel of the town is pure Renaissance. No single element sets this town apart from others, but the harmonious whole is so compelling that Uzès is now designated a national monument.

Attractions

The **aqueduct**, constructed by the Romans around 20 B.C. to bring water to Nîmes, bridges the River Gard about ten miles south of Uzès on route D981. The **Pont du Gard** may be glimpsed from the roadway, but the most impressive view is from the river where it flows beneath the bridge.

As the original fortifications which surrounded the city in medieval times have long since been replaced by a boulevard, the only surviving mementos from the 11th to 14th centuries are three of the towers at **Le Duché** and the **Tour Fenestrelle**, the only part of the original 12th-century cathedral spared by the 16th-century Wars of Religion.

Nîmes is easily reached by using route D979, a lovely 15-mile drive on a country road that is not heavily traveled—most people use D981, with a stop at Pont du Gard.

Hotels

We enjoyed our stay at the **Hôtel St.-Géniès** (Route St.-Ambroix). It is small, without a restaurant, but it's easy to find north of town on route D979. Rates: 295-340F ($59-69), with free parking. Phone: 66-22-29-99.

If, unlike us, you manage to find open rooms in town, try the **Hôtel d'Entraigues** (8, rue de la Calade), a transformed 15th-century manor, with completely modern conveniences. There are marvelous views of the River Eute from the upper stories and a good restaurant for hotel guests. Rates: 320-450F ($64-90), with parking 50F ($10). Phone: 66-22-32-68.

Restaurants

The restaurant at the hotel **d'Agoult/Château d'Arpaillargues** (Arpaillargues, route D982, in the direction of Bagnols) lies a bit out of town, and both the hotel and restaurant are pricey. Menus: 210F ($42) and up. Phone: 66-22-14-48.

Another recommended out-of-town restaurant is the **Auberge St.-Maximin** (in the village of St.-Maximin on route D981, in the direction of Alès). Closed November through April. Menus: 150-190F ($30-38). Phone: 66-22-26-41.

In town, **L'Alexandry** (6, blvd. Gambetta) offers standard French cuisine. Menus: 150-250F ($30-50). Phone: 66-22-27-82.

Chapter 5

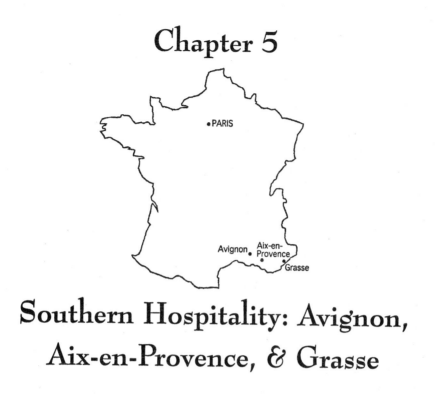

Southern Hospitality: Avignon, Aix-en-Provence, & Grasse

The following morning, we returned to Uzès to meander through the streets, absorbing the sounds and aromas of the awakening town. Although we had breakfasted at the hotel—it is common for hotels without dining facilities to still serve *le petit déjeuner*—we could not resist the enticing smell of fresh-baked bread and robust coffee. From the vantage point of a sidewalk café's terrace, we watched the shopkeepers along the street as they scrubbed the sidewalks clean of the previous day's litter—a custom which could well be emulated by merchants in the United States.

As we sat enjoying our second breakfast, a small, brown dog of uncertain ancestry came bounding up the steps toward us. In

France, dogs are accorded the status of favored children and are freely admitted to restaurants and many hotels as part of the client's family. The surprising thing about this dog was his self-assured air of purpose as he pranced from table to table, giving each occupant a brief inspection before he moved on, seemingly to find a table that better suited his tastes. He bounced onto a chair at the table adjoining ours, sat erect, and turned his head slightly in a quizzical manner, as though to ask, "Where's the waiter?"

"Hi, Cutie," Wendy said. "Are you lost?" Her question was answered almost immediately, as a rather heavy gentleman grunted his way up the stairs and took a seat next to the dog. *"Bonjour, madame et monsieur."* His was the customary greeting all French use when first coming in proximity to others, even strangers.

"Bonjour, monsieur," we responded in unison, but his attention had been transferred to the dog, who quivered with pleasure as the man scratched him behind the ears. It seemed that any further socializing was not encouraged.

A waiter appeared, carrying a tray of croissants along with coffee service for two. With a flourish, accompanied by some rapid repartee which we could not understand, he placed one of the large cups before the dog and the other in front of the man. In what was obviously a long-standing routine, the man proceeded to serve them both, alternately pouring coffee and milk until both cups were filled to his satisfaction. All the while, the dog sat quietly, watching the preparation studiously, showing no sign of impatience. Both man and dog seemed caught in a ceremonious rapture as monsieur peeled the flaky crust from a croissant and dipped it in the dog's cup. The dog remained motionless, with only a short, high-pitched whine to reveal his excitement, as the man moved the dripping pastry toward him *"Vas,"* the man commanded, and the dog lunged forward to claim his reward. The man withdrew his empty hand, counted the fingers, and rewarded himself with the soft, buttery interior of the peeled croissant and a sip of coffee.

The ritual continued until the plate of croissants was exhausted and the last of the coffee was drunk. Then the man stood and brushed the crumbs from his paunch. "*Reste,*" he said sharply when the dog showed signs of leaving the chair. The man slowly walked into the café to settle his bill. The animal's eyes followed his master, but otherwise he remained obediently stationary.

When the man returned, I looked up and remarked admiringly, "*Quel bon chien!*"

"*Elle est ma bonne compagne.*" The words were accompanied by the hint of a smile, but he quickly regained his aloof demeanor. "*Viens,*" he said to the dog, and the two walked away. Just as they reached the steps, the man turned his head and said, "*Au revoir, madame et monsieur.*" Again, there was the trace of a smile.

"That was sweet," Wendy said. "I wonder what they're like at home. Do you suppose he's married?"

"Doubtful," I said, wishing that we could speak French well enough to really establish friendly contacts with fellow human beings, rather than just to satisfy basic needs. Maybe some day.

After that second breakfast, we felt the need for some exercise before resuming our journey to Vence. We followed the inner wall of the city, stopping for a moment to admire the ducal palace and the golden-tiled coat of arms that gleamed in the early morning light. The terraced area of the cathedral was practically deserted, giving us the chance to absorb the view in a moment of quiet isolation. One could almost feel the presence of visitors from the past: Roman soldiers, the popes and bishops, perhaps even the duke himself, all might have stood on this same ground, watching the sun put highlights on the valley below. We walked down the stairway and into a lovely wooded park of tall chestnuts and oaks. A pair of magpies, high in an oak, querulously took note of our presence as we strolled along the path circling the base of the old wall. We reached the car, refreshed and ready for new adventures.

Our route now lay across the wide Rhone River at Avignon, then south through the heart of the Midi to Aix-en-Provence. Here we could stop for lunch, with plenty of time in the afternoon to reach Vence. We arrived in Avignon by mid-morning and parked near the Papal Palace for a bit of sightseeing in this historic city that has thrived since long before the Romans came.

After the fall of Rome, Avignon was ravaged by barbarians and held for a time by Saracen armies before it gained the protection of the French. Disputes in the Vatican led the first French Pope, Clement V, to seek the more hospitable climate of his homeland, where he had the Palais des Papes constructed in 1309. It is a massive fortress, complete with towers, reinforced gates, and battlements from which boiling oil could be poured upon the heads of those who dared trespass against the Holy See. What bloody times those must have been, when even the holiest patriarch of the Christian world had to think like a warrior.

The 20th century has overtaken Avignon, with unfortunate results. Only four graceful arches remain of the Pont d'Avignon, about which French classes still sing, and the Rhone is now bridged with steel girders and cables. When we were there, the dusty path leading from the parking area was dominated by scruffy panhandlers, who sprawled in the dirt beside the palace wall, their pleas for money scrawled on scraps of cardboard. The only one who seemed enterprising enough to offer anything in exchange for the money was playing a sad little tune on a battered flute. His sign beside the open flute case said simply, *"J'ai faim."* In deference to his hunger, I dropped a couple of francs in the case, and we moved on.

The enormous square in front of the palace was filled with stalls and milling people. Another flea market was in progress. I felt somehow cheated, as though something indefinably precious had been taken from me by the commercialization of the historic spot. We worked our way through the crowd to the palace steps to gaze upwards at the imposing battlements. "Do you like this?" Wendy asked.

"No," I complained, "too crowded." Even as the words left my mouth, I realized how petulant I must have sounded. A real "ugly American," I thought. We were guests in a foreign country, permitted to take part in the everyday life of its citizens, and I was feeling cheated because they were going about their usual business. France is not a museum. It is a thriving, vibrant, living country that honors the past, but refuses to live in it. Still, it's easy enough to think like that in the abstract, but quite another thing when you are being jostled from all sides. "It's okay—I've seen enough," I added. "Let's head south."

Easier said than done. Avignon's strategic location makes it the hub of a maze of roads that radiate in all directions. Route designations are not shown by number on road signs, only the name of the large city that lies somewhere down the road is given. Often, too, there is little distance between the sign and the turnoff. Alès, Orange, Nîmes—all sped by in rapid succession, until at last we made the turn toward Aix-en-Provence. This was no tree-lined, two-lane, picturesque country road for the casual motorist; this was a modern expressway that had cautionary signs warning drivers not to exceed the 120-kilometer-per-hour speed limit. As is often the case, the speed limit was taken to mean the slowest speed that one should drive, and even with the speedometer at 120, most of the traffic easily passed us.

It was a relief to turn off the highway at Aix shortly after noon, to forget defending the fenders and instead to give proper attention to the stomach. Aix-en-Provence is the city that meets everyone's ideal of Provençal living—relaxed contentment under a warm sun in a land of bountiful food and good wine. Despite the pressure of a population explosion after World War II, which saw the city grow from 30,000 to its present 130,000, the baroque charm remains.

Aix is a beautiful old city, with flowers planted wherever a bare patch of ground is available. Particularly impressive is the intricate geometric design of the plantings at place de Gaulle, an enormous roundabout that swings cars into the cours Mirabeau. The cours is a broad avenue, shaded by tall, spreading plane trees, lined on one side by picturesque rows of 17th- and 18th-century townhouses and on the other with smart shops and cafés. Aix has become a university town, drawing students from all over the world, particularly during the summer months when students can receive credit for a few weeks of residence while they perfect their French.

Parking was impossible along the cours Mirabeau, but we found a spot about two blocks away. Just enough of a walk to work out the tensions of driving so we could enjoy a relaxed meal. We actually spent more time perusing the menus posted outside the cafés, trying to decide which sounded best, than we had in walking from the car. Finally we settled down at an outside table beneath one of the plane trees and ordered lunch.

Wendy had the Aix equivalent of a chef's salad: lettuce mixed with tomatoes, olives, artichoke hearts, and strips of sweet red pepper, garnished with substantial slices of tender ham. I was more daring and ordered the *rouget à la niçoise*, a chunky fish that probably weighed less than a pound, grilled and served on a bed of tarragon-flavored tomatoes, all topped with slices of lemon alternating with fillets of anchovies. Too late, I remembered that *niçoise* was practically synonymous with anchovies, those salty, unctuous strips of concentrated fishiness, so strong that only horseradish could override the flavor. Wendy watched with amusement as I surreptitiously maneuvered the offending fillets to the tail of the fish. "Next time, try the salad," she advised.

"Hummmph," I muttered as I cut through the crisp, slightly charred pink skin to reveal the moist flesh within. The aroma of the tarragon and tomato was irresistible, and I forked a large portion into my mouth. While the flavor and texture were similar to freshwater black bass, the subtle seasoning changed it from a campsite dish into one that could hold its own in a three-star restaurant. This was a dish to remember.

After lunch, we spent an hour or so wandering through the old section of town that stretched north from the cours to the Cathédrale de Saint-Sauveur. Although it had been built during the same period as the magnificent Gothic cathedrals of the north, it employed the architecture of Rome and, for all of its size, seemed squatty and uninteresting. Nearby, the Atelier de Cézanne was closed, so we were unable to see the restored studio of Paul Cézanne, the most famous artist to be born in Aix-en-Provence. Reason enough for a future visit to that charming city, we thought as we returned to the car to resume our journey.

Vence lies to the north of Nice and to the east of Grasse, giving us an easy choice between the high-speed freeway to the Riviera and the slower country road to Grasse. We arrived at Grasse, hot and thirsty from the drive across the rolling countryside. It had been an uneventful trip, through rustic villages and past old farmhouses on low hills, above fields of sunflowers, corn, or wheat, and occasionally, a small vineyard. Dark, swirling cypress trees were like exclamation marks against the muted ochers and faded browns of the old buildings. We felt as though the road led directly through a painting by Van Gogh or Cézanne.

As we approached Grasse, the hills began to be replaced by more massive formations. We were leaving Provence and entering the Alpes-Maritimes. Heather now covered the steeper slopes, and along their bases, the flatter land was planted in groves of olive and citrus trees. The hot afternoon air was infused with the scent of orange blossoms and lavender from the fields that supplanted the heather on the lower slopes.

Grasse is set on a southern slope, surrounded by the pastel patchwork fields of pink heather and lavender. The city is built on several broad terraces, like the seats of some giant amphitheater from which the ancient gods could watch the epic struggles of Ulysses on the broad stage of the distant Mediterranean. This is the town where Napoleon Bonaparte visited his sister, Pauline, while she recovered her health and the site of the Plateau Napoleon, which commemorates the spot where the Emperor picnicked.

We arrived hot and thirsty and parked the car near Napoleon's picnic ground, in a long, narrow park called the Jeu de Ballon, which boasts a fast-food restaurant under sheltering plane trees. We ordered beer and *jus de pamplemousse avec glaçons*—grapefruit juice with ice cubes—and settled back to enjoy the magnificent view. Although the air was hazy, we imagined that we could see the Mediterranean across the balustrade that kept the unwary from plunging over the precipice. "Why don't we stay here tonight?" Wendy asked. "Vence is so small that we might not get a room there."

One of the advantages of traveling without itinerary or reservations is the ability to change as whim or circumstance may dictate. The ever-reliable tourist office found us a room at a hotel, very close to the Jeu de Ballon, so we did not have to move the car. I also filled my pocket with brochures about the city and its many attractions. Two were from perfume distilleries that offered free tours of their plants so that we could follow the process of reducing flowers to essence; another had a map of the city, with restaurant locations marked with bold Xs. Most interesting to me was the brochure from the Musée de Fragonard, which promised some of the best works by the locally born painter.

We settled into the hotel, leaving Old Gray to spend the night alone in the car, and set out to follow the map of the restaurants. Two were located on a large square, about two blocks from the hotel, but the map did not indicate that the square was on the lower terrace of the town, to be reached only by an unmarked flight of stairs. After several minutes of confused walking, in desperation I stopped a pedestrian and, in my jumbled French, asked, *"Pardonez moi, monsieur. Où se trouve cette place?"* I showed him the map and pointed with my finger at the large X, placed there by the woman at the tourist bureau.

He gave me a penetrating look, as if to be certain that he had my full attention, then, with the relish of a master imparting wisdom on a novice, replied *"C'est là-bas."* As he spoke, he half turned and grandly gestured to the stairway. He waited until we were safely on the stairs before he resumed his walk. After all, one can't be too careful when giving directions to foreigners.

The stairs led to a large square, paved with cobblestones and enclosed on all four sides by ancient buildings. On the side from which we entered, there stretched a solid wall of small shops on the ground level, with shuttered residences on the second floors, backed against the hillside. Across the way, the entrances to several narrow alleys invited exploration. We stepped into one and were met by the cool, musty smell of ancient habitation. We looked down to where the passage curved and marveled at the way a tall, half-timbered structure had been built to follow the curve of the path. It seemed probable that the rectangular square and the surrounding buildings were from the original town, with the area above representing 17th-century additions as the perfume industry prospered.

A little exploring of dark alleys can go a long way, so we decided to check out the restaurants. The first, judging from the menu posted on the door, was more of a fast steak-and-french-fry place than a proper restaurant. We trudged the length of the square to where the second was supposed to be, only to find a sign with the name "Vieux Bistrot" printed on it, along with an arrow that pointed down the sloping ramp of another alley. "What do you think?" I asked skeptically.

"Let's go for it." Wendy started down the alley. We found the Vieux Bistrot at the first turn, where the alley joined with another and widened slightly to form a small courtyard. The menu offered roast pork, breast of duck, and *salmon en cruit*, along with soup and assorted hors d'oeuvres. We looked into the darkened interior of the place, but there seemed to be no one there.

"*Il-y-a personne?*" I called.

A door opened in the rear, spilling light into the room. The man wore a white cap and apron over a T-shirt and blue jeans. I noticed that he was wearing sandals and thought it an open invitation to disaster should a sauce begin to splatter.

"*Vous désirez?*" he asked.

"*Je voudrais,*" I started out, but the proper French construction deserted me. "Reservation?" I ended lamely.

"Ah, you want dinner tonight?"

I nodded my head in agreement.

"Eight o'clock," the man said. "We start at eight o'clock."

"Our names?" I asked. "Don't you need our names?"

"No," he said with a sly look, "I will remember you."

So, we were set for dinner, but my watch showed that it was barely seven o'clock, meaning dinner was a long hour off. "We could go back to the park and watch the sunset," I ventured.

"Let's just go back to the square and look in windows. Maybe we can find someplace to sit down."

That sounded fine to me, especially the part about sitting, so we wandered back into the square, idly looking in the shop windows until the tables and chairs in front of the *crêperie* invited us to sit. "We could split one," Wendy offered, knowing that it would spoil dinner, but her thoughts were on her tired feet and a chair.

So, we sat down and found that along with all manner of crêpes and *gallantins*, bottled cider from Brittany was offered. "We really should drink more liquids in this hot weather," Wendy advised. We settled for one plate of crêpes, filled with tiny wild strawberries and sour cream, and a liter of cold cider. The crêpes, of course, disappeared immediately, but we were permitted to nurse the bottle along until it was nearly eight o'clock.

When we returned to the restaurant, we were surprised to find that tables to accommodate about twenty people were set in the small courtyard area. Light was provided by a string of brightly colored lanterns, although each table had a candle burning within a glass chimney placed alongside a small bud vase with sprigs of heather and lavender. The glassware and silver sparkled against the starched white of the table covers and napkins. A young couple sat at a table in the far corner, totally absorbed in one another, while a hidden loudspeaker was quietly playing some harp music. It looked like the setting for a garden party or wedding reception.

Our host, now without his apron and cap, showed us to a small table next to the restaurant wall. "You will not be disturbed here," he said in a reassuring tone. "Would you like a *kir* while you wait?"

Kir, a bit of cassis in white wine, sounded like a splendid way to introduce dinner, and we quickly assented. He brought the drinks, along with menus, then hurried to seat an arriving party of four at a large table across the alley from us. The well-dressed foursome was obviously in a party mood and paid us little attention as they carried on a light-hearted banter in spirited French. The *maître d'hôtel* brought them a bottle of champagne, which he carefully opened and served before returning to his station where a number of people had appeared.

It was eight o'clock, the appointed hour. In a whirlwind of motion, our host assigned his guests to the remaining tables. Two women were placed in front of the young couple that had arrived first; a group of six boisterous Italians was accommodated at the largest table near the entrance; and another couple was seated at the table in front of us. A single woman with a small boy was escorted through the maze of tables and chairs to the far end, where they proceeded up the alley, presumably to their home. The whole maneuver was accomplished with the adroitness of a stage manager for the café scene from "La Bohème."

As the last of the tables were filled, a waiter appeared. The tall, skinny young man with a black bow tie, aided by the host, efficiently took orders from all the guests. The music abandoned the ethereal harp and switched to a tape of American movie-soundtracks that seemed to better fit the festive scene as the hors d'oeuvres arrived. Artistically arranged plates of lobster ravioli with strips of flame-roasted sweet red peppers were set before us. The skillful service was broken only momentarily by the appearance of an older man, jauntily waving a loaf of bread as he worked his way through the jumble of tables and up the alley on his way home.

We had barely time to finish the luscious lobster when the music changed again. The rock beat continued, but the tune and subtle harmonics sounded vaguely familiar. The Italian table was first to recognize it and, with screams of laughter, its occupants pointed upward. There, creeping over the rim of the building to a modernized version of "Clair de Lune," was the shining face of a full moon. We felt that we'd joined a merry band of revelers on a festive barge, floating down a gentle river under a harvest moon.

The enchantment of the moment was quickly broken as fresh gales of laughter returned our eyes to the Italian table. There, a seemingly impossible feat was being attempted. An enormous motorcycle was poised to make its way through the narrow passage. Good-naturedly, one of the diners had set himself in front of the machine and was energetically moving tables and chairs aside, while the others had formed a serpentine line behind, fitting a conga dance step to this upbeat version of "Clair de Lune." The carnival parade threaded its way to the end of the dining area before it bid adieu to the Harley and broke up, its component couples returning to their tables amid continuing laughter.

The entrées arrived: duck breast with prunes and lemon for Wendy, roast pork in calvados for me. A lovely bottle of Côtes de Beaune had replaced the glasses of *kir* and complemented both dishes admirably. The small green beans and slices of summer squash that accompanied the meats were still crisp and had been lightly touched with rosemary and lavender, imparting the impression that we were eating the sweet-scented air of Provence.

A chilled salad of tiny lettuce leaves, sprinkled with a piquant vinaigrette, was followed by a cheese plate. After sampling the *plateau de fromages*, which called for the last of the wine, we were ready for dessert. Fresh raspberries were piled high on a base of bittersweet chocolate, all topped with thick whipped cream and flavored by a dash of kirsch. Wendy looked at me with dismay, but gamely took up her spoon. We realized that we would do penance in the morning, but it was just too good to leave untouched. Both desserts were totally consumed before the coffee arrived.

The final surprise of the evening began with the dynamic opening chords of Johann Strauss' "Gold and Silver Waltz." After the first few bars, a rock beat was subtly interwoven with the waltz, producing a sense of being slightly off balance. Then, at first only a few, flashing briefly like wounded moths in candlelight, a cloud of thin paper discs the size of two-franc coins began to flutter down from above, glistening in the lantern light like oversized gold-and-silver snowflakes. Looking up, we could see our host leaning out of the topmost window, waving gaily as he tossed the confetti into the air. The applause was spontaneous, transcending all language in appreciation for the magic of that moonlit evening in an alley in Grasse.

~ On Your Own ~

Avignon

Avignon's strategic location on the banks of the Rhone meant that it could not avoid history, nor can the visitor here. The Romans used this major north-south waterway in their expansion to the north, and fifteen centuries later the Church of Rome followed suit and built the Palais des Papes in the walled city. Now, it makes a good place from which to make exploratory trips into the surrounding areas of Provence.

Attractions

From mid-July to mid-August, Avignon is crowded with visitors to the **Festival d'Art Dramatique et de Danse**, an off-the-wall celebration of the newest in film, drama, and dance. The town numbers about 90,000 inhabitants, but at festival time it is estimated that as many as 250,000 spectators crowd its streets; not a good time to be looking for a hotel.

The **Palais des Papes** was stripped of its elaborate decorations and luxuriant furnishings following the end of the Great Schism and the return of the Papacy to Rome in 1417. Your imagination will have to furbish the enormous, gloomy halls in a manner befitting the man who was the most powerful on earth. For 22F ($4.50) you can take an unguided tour of the palace or pay 30F ($6) for one with a guide. Phone: 90-86-03-32.

The **Pont d'Avignon** (actually the Pont St.-Bénezet) has been reduced to only four of its original twenty-two arches by centuries of Rhone floods. Although the dancing may be precarious, you can still walk upon the remaining span while you hum the song, "*Sur le pont d'Avignon, on y danse . . .* "

Near the palace, within the 12th-century **Cathédrale de Notre-Dame**, you can view the elaborate tomb of Pope John XXII and the contrastingly chaste tomb of Pope Benedict XII. The gilded statue over the tombs was added in the 19th century.

The **Musée du Petit-Palais** is full of religious paintings from Renaissance Italy, along with some rooms containing Roman and Gothic sculptures from the Avignon area. Tickets are 18F ($3.60). Closed Tuesdays. Phone: 90-86-44-58.

Beyond the immediate palace area on the place de l'Horloge you will find the Théâtre and the Hôtel de Ville. Further along is Avignon's most interesting museum, the **Musée Calvet** (65, rue Joseph-Vernet). Inside you will find a pot-pourri of items beyond an avid collector's dreams and a museum director's nightmares: tapestries and Renaissance furniture, an Egyptian mummy, Roman cooking pots, wrought iron from the 16th to 18th centuries, and paintings that range in style from Dutch still-lifes to Utrillos and Dufys. A tour of the 18th-century mansion and its lovely courtyard alone would be worth the price of admission, 20F ($4). Closed Tuesdays. Phone: 90-86-33-84.

In the surrounding area:

Nîmes contains some of the best-preserved mementos from the days of Rome. The 1st-century *arènes* (**arena**) is still in use today for rock concerts, or with matadors and bulls substituting for the gladiators of old. The **Maison Carrée** is the graceful Roman temple that inspired Thomas Jefferson in his designs for Monticello and, to a less successful degree, the architects of the bulky Madeleine in Paris. The city, filled with many more admission-free delights, is only 25 miles from Avignon. Take route N100 west across the river to the well-marked route N86 south, in the direction of Nîmes.

Arles, another repository of Roman antiquities, lies 22 miles south of Avignon. Its **arena**, the largest in Provence, stages bull fights during the summer, and the adjoining Roman **theater**, which has been repaired enough to be functional, stages an annual drama festival in July. Admission to the arena (phone: 90-96-03-70) is 17F ($3.50) and to the theater (phone: 90-96-93-30), not for a production, the charge is 12F ($2.40). Route N570 leads directly south from Avignon to Arles.

Orange (18 miles north of Avignon on route N7) has two Roman antiquities of special note: the **triumphal arch**, echoed by l'Arc de Triomphe in Paris, and the **theater** which dates from the time of Augustus. The hillside theater once seated 8,000 people on stone tiers rising above the stage. The acoustics remain so good, that even today a whisper from the stage may be heard on the highest tier. Phone: 90-51-80-06.

St-Rémy has become a place of pilgrimage for the lovers of Vincent van Gogh, although there is little to see beyond the plain, stucco building that once housed the tormented artist (phone: 90-92-02-31). Head south from Avignon for about a mile on N570 before turning off onto route D571; St-Rémy is about 12 miles from there.

Les Baux lies an additional five miles from St-Rémy and is worth the trip. Like the "Hole in the Wall" gang of the U.S. West, the brigands of Les Baux scourged the countryside, safe from reprisal in their mountain fortress. In 1632, Richelieu brought the full might of the French army against Les Baux, destroying the castle and ramparts. Today, the site rates three stars from Michelin, as does the restaurant **l'Oustau de Beaumaniere** (phone: 90-54-33-07) located in the valley below Les Baux.

Beaucaire and Tarascon lie facing each other across the Rhone, the former with only fragile remnants of its past while **Tarascon** has the best-preserved castle in France. Built in the 15th century, the castle, **Château du Roi René**, was the residence of the last king of an independent Provence. Although the exterior is properly menacing as befits a fortress, the interior is a curious mixture of styles, combining flamboyant Gothic with Renaissance to make a home suitable for a king. Turn off route N570 leading to Arles onto route D970 to Tarascon.

Hotels

Bristol-Terminus (44, cours Jean-Jaurès, Avignon) may not have a restaurant, but in the overheated days of summer you'll appreciate its superior air conditioning. Closed in February. Rates: 500F ($100), parking 50F ($10). Phone: 90-82-21-21.

Angleterre (29, blvd. Raspail, Avignon) is small and lacking a restaurant, but very reasonably priced. Closed from December 15 to January 15. Rates: 240-350F ($48-70), with free parking! Phone: 90-86-34-31.

Midi (53, rue République, Avignon) is also small and without a restaurant and likewise quite affordable. Closed from December 10 to January 25. Rates: 300-450F ($60-90). Phone: 90-82-15-56.

Restaurants

Avignon has its share of Michelin-rated one- and two-star restaurants, but all require advance reservations. The following restaurants are less-pretentious establishments serving good food at reasonable prices.

Le Petit Bédon (70, rue Joseph-Vernet) is always busy and will seat no one after 10:30 pm, so it is best to arrive early. Closed Sundays and the last two weeks of June. There are menus for under 250F ($50). Phone: 90-82-33-98.

Le Corail (64, blvd. St-Roch) serves typical Provençal food, with lots of olive oil and garlic. Closed Sundays. Menus: 100-150F ($20-30). Phone: 90-27-03-26.

As in Paris, often the best meal is a simple *plat du jour* served on the terrace of a *brasserie*. There are several cafés and *brasseries* clustered around the **place de l'Horloge** and the **place des Corps-Saints**.

Aix-en-Provence

Aix is a city of fountains. In fact, its name is derived from the 2nd-century Roman outpost built over the natural springs in the area, commanded by Caius Sextius Calvinus. The name "Aquae Sextiae," over the next millennium, became contracted to "Aix" (pronounced "X"). Every square has its own refreshing fountain, and if you do nothing more than walk slowly from one to the next, observing the variety of shops set in the context of beautifully preserved architecture from the 16th to 17th centuries, you will always fondly remember Aix.

Attractions

Aix is particularly crowded during the last three weeks of July when the annual **Festival of Music** is staged. Tickets for the events (mostly classical) are expensive and limited.

The Roman general's name remains in its uncorrupted state on the only mineral-water spring in town, the **Thermes Sextius**.

The **Musée des Tapisseries** is housed in what was once a palace of the archbishops, and is now also one of the sites of the music festival.

The tapestries on exhibit are not the ordinary run-of-the-castle draft-stoppers, but were beautifully crafted during the 17th and 18th centuries on order from the archbishops to decorate the gilded walls of the palace. The "History of Don Quixote" is particularly impressive. Closed Tuesdays and all of January. Admission: 11F ($2.20). Phone: 42-21-05-78.

The **Cathédrale de St.-Sauveur** is hard to appreciate in its entirety. The earliest dating places the baptistry in the 5th century, but it's circled by Roman columns from the 2nd century. Additions were made in various styles throughout the succeeding years, until 1425 when a transept was added along with the completion of the lower tower. Some uniformity was achieved in 1697 when several separate chapels were connected to the transept. A student of architectural history could spend a lifetime here. Phone: 42-23-45-65.

The **Atelier de Cézanne** (just out of town at 9, ave. Paul-Cézanne) has been maintained just as he left it when, in 1906, he died in the town of his birth. There is his coat hanging on the wall, and an unfinished painting still on the easel. Closed Tuesdays. Admission 12F ($2.40). Phone: 42-21-06-53. Farther out of town, route D17 (route de Cézanne) takes you through the countryside between Aix and the village of Le Tholonet where you can see the landscape he often painted.

The **Musée Granet** is the most ambitious museum in Aix, but tries to do too much. In the basement is a display of the archaeological finds from the early Roman settlement, while the upper floor is devoted to a conglomeration of paintings from Italy, Holland, and France, mostly from the 17th through 19th centuries. One monster, "Jupiter and Thetis" by Ingres, is almost lost in the rows upon rows of unremarkable works. Even the self-portrait by Rembrandt is likely to be overlooked in the jumble. Phone: 42-38-14-70.

The **Foundation Vasarely** is actually a museum for the works of the modern artist Vasarely combined with a study center for the arts. Follow the blvd. de la République west out of town across the bridge. You can't miss the startling arrangement of squares and circles in black, white, and gray that stretches along the crest of a hill. Within, you will see some of Vasarely's amazing designs for apartment buildings and his "plastic alphabet," outgrowths of his theories of visual harmony. If you choose not to go in, the drive by is worth the trip. Closed Tuesdays. Admission 25F ($5).

Hotels

Cardinal (24, rue Cardinale), situated three blocks south of cours Mirabeau near the Musée Granet, has rooms furnished after the manner of country inns. Rates: 330-380F ($66-76), parking 40F ($8). Phone: 42-38-32-30.

Moderne (34, ave. Victor-Hugo) is conveniently located near the tourist office at place du Général de Gaulle at the base of cours Mirabeau. Rates: 370-450F ($74-90), parking 40F ($8). Phone: 42-26-05-16.

Globe (74, cours Sextius) is near the mineral springs on the north side of town; it may be somewhat faded now, but it's still a good value. Closed from December 23 through the end of January. Rates: 360-400F ($72-80). Phone: 42-26-03-58.

Restaurants

Les Clam's (22, cours Sextius) is the place for seafood. Located near the center of the old town, it is an easy walk to cours Mirabeau to ease that overstuffed feeling. Menus: 200-240F ($40-48). Phone: 42-27-64-78.

Chez Maxime (12, place Ramus) specializes in the cuisine of Provence, offering such fare as a cassolette of mussels, beef with truffle sauce, and barbecued lamb. Menus: 120-160F ($24-40). Closed Sundays and all of February. Phone: 42-26-28-51.

The **Brasserie Royal** (17, cours Mirabeau) has one section which is designated "restaurant," but the only significant difference is in the pricing. Sit under the awning which stretches above the sidewalk and watch the passing parade as you dine at a reduced price. Menus: 100-150F ($20-30). Phone: 42-26-01-63.

Grasse

Grasse is a lovely city from which to explore the delights of southeastern Provence and the Côte d'Azur. For those who fancy sun and skin, major highways provide fast access to Cannes (N85) and Nice (D2085), and for those of a more contemplative nature, numerous back roads lead to hilltop villages which still retain the character of centuries past. Perfume, after 300 years, is still the essence of life in Grasse, and the acres of flowers on the hillsides surrounding the city will add to your enjoyment.

Attractions

The **Parfumerie Fragonard** (in the center of town at 20, blvd. Fragonard) offers a free tour with an English-speaking guide to explain the intricacies of extracting *l'âme de la fleur* ("the soul of the flower"). Open daily, even holidays. Phone: 93-36-44-65.

The **Musée d'Art et d'Histoire de Provence** contains a vast amount of material ranging from archeological finds, through home furnishings and utensils from past eras, to paintings. Open daily through the summer months, but closed all of November, and on Mondays and Tuesdays in October and December through May. Admission is 12.60F ($2.50). Phone: 93-36-01-61.

The once **Cathédrale de Notre-Dame** (now a mere *église*) combines Lombard and early Gothic styles, but still looks typically Romanesque. The painting herein, "Christ Washing the Disciples' Feet," is the only known example of Fragonard's religious paintings.

In the surrounding area:

Saint-Vallier-de-Thiey lies about seven miles north of Grasse and is one of the oldest villages in Provence. Surrounded by a medieval wall, it gives no hint of its origins as the Roman settlement of Castrum Valerii. Take N85 in the direction of Castellane.

If ruined castles are your thing, there is a splendid example with a marvelous view of the countryside at **Cabris**, just four miles west of Grasse on route D4. The chapel is from the late 14th century, but the church is 17th-century.

Saint-Cézaire-sur Siagne, nine miles west of Grasse off route D2562, still looks like a medieval village should. It is dominated by three 14th-century towers and protected by its original town gate.

Mougins lies equidistant between Grasse and Cannes. The wealthy come here from Cannes for the fine golf course.

Hotels

At **Panorama** (2, place du Cours, Grasse) a room with a view will cost extra, but even those lacking a balcony have a bath. Rates: 395-460F ($79-92). Phone: 93-36-80-802.

Bellevue (14, ave. Riou-Blanquet, Grasse) is an old but serviceable hotel on the high ground in the old city. Closed all of November. Rates: 225-400F ($45-80). Phone: 93-36-01-96.

Restaurants

Le Vieux Bistrot is the delightful place in Grasse which provided us with such a memorable time; menus: 125-200F ($25-40). The little alley, rue de Moulinets, opens onto one end of rue Fabrières, and **La Galerie Gourmand** lies at the opposite end. In between is the **Crêperie Bretonne**, where the a la carte menu can be a pleasant change from the standard heavy fare. All are closed Sundays.

The **Amphitryon** (16, blvd Victor-Hugo, Grasse) serves the best food in town, but it is closed Sundays, the first week in April, all of August, Christmas through New Year's Day, and all major holidays. Menus: 162-242F ($32-48). Phone: 93-36-58-73.

Serving typical Provençal fare, the **Maître Boscq** (13, rue Fontette, Grasse) is closed Sundays and holidays, and from June 29 until July 6. Menus: 110-160F ($22-32). Phone: 93-36-45-76.

Chapter 6

La Comédie Rustique: Vence, Marseille, & the Côte d'Azur

The back road from Grasse to Vence climbed past stone farm-houses with red-tiled roofs, encircled by dusty groves of silver-leafed olive trees, their knotted trunks revealing an ageless vitality. A few miles farther, and we were traveling through dense wooded areas, past trellised orchards of pears and figs, over crag-gy ridges and half around the spectacular medieval village of Tourrette-sur-Loup, perched high above the Loup River.

Arriving at Vence is almost a letdown after such a scenic drive. Although Vence was established by the Romans as a base camp, little remains from those early days: the town has become a commercial center for the processing and selling of olive oil. For the tourist, the chief attractions are La Chapelle du Rosaire, the small, exquisite chapel designed and decorated by Henri Matisse, and the proximity of the reconstructed mountaintop village of Saint-Paul-de-Vence.

We planned to spend the night in the *auberge* Closerie des Genêts, a charming inn with a superb restaurant, located just off the main town square. We had stayed there on a previous trip when we first explored the Riviera and were looking forward to enjoying this return visit. However, all of the parking near the square was occupied, so we followed the signs directing us to another parking area that lay about three blocks away, on the outskirts of town. While I searched for the *compteur* to buy a ticket for parking, Wendy stood beside the car, surveying the scene. When I returned, she was obviously distressed. "How could they?" she said. "Look where we are." She pointed toward the low wall at the far end of the lot. "A cemetery!"

"So? They have to put it somewhere." I couldn't see what was so upsetting about a few rows of weeping angels, cherubs, and assorted crosses.

"Look across the street." Her eyes, narrowed with indignation, were fixedly staring over my shoulder.

The object of Wendy's wrath looked like a typical resort hotel, five or six floors high, each room with a sliding glass door leading onto a balcony. Lounge chairs, evenly spaced along the balconies, were for the most part occupied by people enjoying the early morning sun. The only movement was from white-dressed attendants who were trundling more people onto the balconies . . . frail, silvery haired people who had to be lifted from wheelchairs. This was a home for aged, infirm pensioners, with little enough to look forward to in life, now given a cemetery to look out upon. My own age, to which I usually give little thought, seemed to take on additional significance.

"I don't think that I can ever stay here again," Wendy said. "I'd dream about those poor people."

"Okay," I said, abandoning any thought of changing her mind. "Let's take off for the Maeght in Saint-Paul-de-Vence. We can find something for the night on down the coast."

St.-Paul-de-Vence has been taken over by the artistic set, and its restoration has made it one of the most beautiful of all the Mediterranean hilltop villages. However, since we had decided not to stay in Vence, we settled on spending our available time locally at the Foundation Maeght—a museum of modern art that's always worth a special detour to see. Coming up from the parking lot, through a grove of olive trees, the visitor's attention is caught by the strong, primary colors of a huge stabile by Alexander Calder mounted in front of the entrance. Inside, within a large, glass-enclosed courtyard which forms the inner walls of the museum, are gaunt, elongated, bronze figures by Alberto Giacometti, seemingly frozen in mid-stride. An entire wall is given to mosaics by Marc Chagall, and a large rock garden forms a perfect setting for ceramics by Joan Miro.

Still, no matter how lovely the setting or how dramatic the displays, there is something inherent in a museum that generates a desire to be elsewhere, a desire that is exponentially proportional to the length of time spent in the museum. After about an hour of assimilating culture, the urge to resume our wandering had reached irresistible proportions. We left the Foundation Maeght without any idea of where we were going, but energized by the prospects of the open road.

The roads here have been widened to accommodate all the commuters to Nice from the reconstructed mountain villages such as St.-Paul-de-Vence and Tourrette-sur-Loup. France is becoming more like the United States, with jobs in the cities and stylish living in the suburbs. We arrived in the outskirts of Nice within twenty minutes, and I pulled into the parking lot of a large shopping center that could have been lifted out of any town at home. "I thought a picnic might be fun," I said, answering Wendy's questioning look.

The supermarket featured a few notable differences from its counterparts in the United States: the wine section occupied about one-third of the store; all weights and sizes were in metric units; and all of the produce was very fresh, and the fruit was fully ripened. We loaded a basket with heavy red tomatoes, fragrant peaches, and a small cantaloupe from Provence. A wedge of brie, a short length of summer sausage, and a loaf of crusty bread that was heat-sealed in plastic wrap (an unexpected concession to modernity) took care of the remainder of our food. Plastic cups, paper towels, and lastly, a bottle of red wine from the enormous selection, completed our purchases. I was thankful when the total remained on the checkout-counter screen while I produced the correct amount of bills and coins; I knew from past experience that my mind was unable to process 183.75 without seeing it written. The way the French speak, it would have sounded something like, "centquatrevingttresfrancsousantquanz."

Back in the car with our lunch, I looked at the map and reluctantly suggested to Wendy that we break another rule. "If we take the regular roads through all the little beach towns, it will take us all day just to get to Marseille. If we take the *péage*, we could be past Marseille in a couple of hours," I said plaintively. The thought of negotiating through all that traffic in the heat of the Mediterranean sun had melted the last of my explorer's resolve.

"You made the rule," she laughed.

We turned onto the *péage* a few miles farther into the city. The entrance was well marked by a familiar blue overhead sign with the words "Cannes" on top and "Péage" below. Several miles down the road we were stopped by a barricade of toll booths. The booths were unmanned, but contained *compteurs* that dispensed a ticket which gave the time and location when a button was pushed. The ticket would be collected along with the money due when we exited. A very efficient system unless one neglects to take the ticket or loses it before reaching the exit. In those cases, the motorist is charged for the distance from the farthest possible entry point, even though he may have traveled only a few miles.

Again, we found that the posted 120-kilometer signs were taken to indicate the minimum speed, and we whizzed to Cannes without a thought until we came upon the toll collection station stretching across the road. Afterwards, cars freely entered and exited the *péage* for several miles, until we came to yet another bank of ticket dispensers. Apparently, Cannes residents could use that small section of the road as a local interchange without payment.

With a fresh ticket in hand, we left Cannes unexplored; our destination was now Marseille. Our road stretched across the southern tip of Provence in a straight line, bypassing numerous picturesque towns in its quest for speedy efficiency. The country was hilly grassland, with a scattering of oak, poplar, and locust trees growing in the hollows where water was more plentiful. This was grazing land, and small herds of large, cream-colored cattle gathered wherever they could find shade beneath the trees or in the shadows of isolated farm buildings.

Two hours later, we got our first view of Marseille as the *autoroute* swept over a hill and down toward the city. It reminded me of Houston as seen from the air. Extensive estuaries seemed to stretch from the sea right into the city where they disappeared, hidden by rows of tall, modern office buildings. After paying our toll, we left the highway and were engulfed by traffic on a wide avenue named La Canebière—only a city with the reputation of Marseille would have the audacity to call its main street "The Beer Bottle." This was the city that could trace its ancestry back to the time when Phoenicians ruled the Mediterranean, a city that saw the elephants of Hannibal marching on Rome, and a harbor for the latine-rigged African ships that supplied the Moors when they controlled Provence. This was the city that gave its name to the stirring marching song of Napoleon's armies, "La Marseillaise"—a bustling city that is too busy with the present to reminisce about the past.

It took us the better part of a half hour to work our way down La Canebière to the old harbor, which had been modernized only to the level needed to continue its usefulness. It was crowded with pleasure craft and a few fishing boats, but there was no place to park, so we slowly toured the area by car. The fortress, Château d'If, dominated the entrance to the port. This was the prison for political prisoners, made infamous as the site where Alexandre Dumas incarcerated his fictional hero, the Count of Monte Cristo.

Marseille, even more so than Paris, is not a city in which to bring a car. We retraced our route, with each intersection presenting new confusion, as we looked for a sign that would direct us west to Montpellier. There was none: every sign was intent on sending us back to Nice. We backtracked on a parallel street, trying to avoid the heavy traffic, still hoping for a sign that never came.

Despondency had almost turned to desperation when Wendy saw the office of our car rental agency. Even more miraculously, there was a spot to park a short distance away. We wasted no time in asking directions out of the city and on to Montpellier. The young lady explained, in a soothing voice apparently reserved for distraught travelers, that all roads leading from Marseille also lead to Nice, at least until the first bank of ticket machines is reached. There, one is given the choice between Nice and Nîmes. Nîmes, lying to the north, was the one we should select until we reached Arles, where we would be able to choose between Nîmes and Montpellier. It was all so logical that, after her careful explanation, it almost made sense to me.

Still, since we were finally parked, it seemed a waste not to at least have a cool drink, and to answer the inevitable call to nature, before forging on ahead into the ever-warming day. A nearby sidewalk café with a well-kept, yet antique ambience fit the bill.

Like many cafés throughout France, a single toilet at the base of a steep stairway was provided here for the entire establishment. Wendy descended into the unknown depths while I ordered a second round of Pernod to maintain our rights to the table. Several minutes later, she reappeared.

"You won't believe it," she said as she took her seat.

"Dirty?"

"Oh, no. Very clean, but it's like a one-holer on a farm, except that there's no bench."

My turn, and I began my descent on the circular iron stairs that clattered with every step, despite my efforts to be discreet. The steps ended in a box-like hall with a wash basin and a single door marked with the letters "WC." A light push on the door and it swung open to reveal a tiny room. The floor consisted of a circular basin, about five feet in diameter, with two raised steps, one on either side of an eight-inch hole.

I knew that one must stand on the foot rests and position oneself squarely over the hole, all the while trying not to think of any soft, pallid thing with sharp teeth that might be scurrying below. I placed a foot on one of the steps, only to discover that I was facing the wrong way. With arms stretched to brace against the walls, I maneuvered around until both feet were on the appropriate steps, but the door had swung shut, leaving me in utter darkness. It seemed that I could hear the scraping of claws on rock and a sibilant hiss from the hole below.

A panic push and the door was open. With one hand holding the door open, I perched precariously off balance as I searched for the light switch. A pull chain dangled from a water tank above, a square metal container filled with coarse, pink tissue was clamped to the wall, but nowhere was the magic button I needed. My admiration for Wendy increased by logarithmic leaps as I tried to imagine how she had managed without a light.

There was no way I could straddle that hole and hold the door open at the same time. I looked around for something to use as a prop against the door. Nothing. Perhaps Wendy had used her purse? Anything would do. I looked at my feet and the inspiration struck. I removed my left shoe and placed it on the raised sill so that when the door closed, a broad crack allowed the light to seep in. It would do unless someone came along, but I would hear the clatter on the staircase in time to make adjustments.

I finished without interruption and automatically pulled the chain. Water cascaded into the basin like a jet from a fire hose, sloshing against the foot rests and threatening to soak my shoeless left foot. Desperately, I lunged for my shoe, managing only to knock it loose from the door which immediately closed. The darkness was total, and I could still hear the water rising. I pushed my hands against the walls for support and lifted the vulnerable foot from its perch. I stood on one leg, arms outstretched like a wounded flamingo, waiting for the water to subside.

Finally, the torrent abated, and I relaxed, although I could not see to lower my foot. I moved my right hand cautiously along the wall to the corner and then to the door. My fingers brushed the knob that locked the door, and I gave it a slight push. Blessed light streamed in through the opened door, and I lowered my foot to its appointed place just as the door swung shut again. I swung my hand at the door, catching the latch off center, driving the bolt home to lock the door. As it did, it also turned on a light within the toilet chamber.

I cleaned up at the wash basin, replaced my shoe and hurried back to where Wendy sat dawdling with her drink. "Amazing the way the light comes on when you lock the door," I said.

"Ohhhh yeah, I was going to mention that," she replied.

Once out of Marseille and on the road toward Montpellier, having chosen wisely at each point of decision, our high spirits returned. The road followed the coastline, giving us brief glimpses of Martigues and Lavera, old fishing villages that were rapidly being claimed as vacation centers by those wishing a setting more rustic than Cannes or Nice. Then our route turned northward, through the flat, broad delta of the Rhone, until we reached Arles and the end of the *péage*.

The sun seemed to be stopped in its track overhead and blazed down with increasing ferocity as we passed through Saint-Giles, pausing only long enough to espy the ornate facade of a Romanesque church and a single café with tables set out in the full sun. Stopping for a stroll was not very tempting, so it was on to Montpellier or melt.

Despite my normal law-abiding instincts, I found myself pressing down on the accelerator, forcing the car to go faster, faster toward the salvation of Montpellier. We had all of the windows down, but the air was so warm that perspiration dried as it formed on the skin, with no sense of cooling. I sat hunched forward, urging the car along, while Wendy lay limp and semi-comatose in her seat. The engine and the rushing air combined to make conversation impossible, which was fine since neither of us had anything to say. At last, we saw a welcome sign that we had arrived. I swung off the freeway, following the directions to Montpellier airport. "Are we there?" Wendy asked.

"Close enough," I answered. "I'm going to put us up for the night in an air-conditioned Hilton or Sofitel or whatever they have. There's bound to be one near the airport."

We found a Novotel within a block of the turn-off, but it displayed the *C'est Complet* sign at the door, so it was back to the hot car and on down the road. We passed about a mile of enormous buildings displaying such names as IBM, NEC, and Hewlett-Packard, each with its own parking lot filled with cars. Montpellier had obviously become the Silicon Valley of France, so we were not surprised that the next hotel, an Ibis, was also showing a "No Vacancy" sign.

"We'd better go on into town," Wendy suggested. "Those computer companies probably keep the hotels near the airport filled all the time."

So, it was back to the freeway, with five more miles before the next turn-off that lead straight into town. The first stoplight was at an intersection dominated by a large stone building housing the tourist bureau. We pulled in and both of us entered the lovely, air-conditioned room. The heat had grown so intense that we would have gladly spent the evening on a bench in that room, rather than drive on. However, the lady behind the desk was too efficient to permit transient loungers, and we were quickly provided with a fistful of brochures and directions in English to the downtown Sofitel Hotel where she reserved a room for us.

The town was much larger than indicated on the map, but our directions were good, and we found the hotel without difficulty. Although the rate was $150 per night, double the amount we usually hope to pay, the air conditioning alone was worth the extra expense. The lady at the desk provided a small map on which she indicated the location of the nearest places to eat. There was a large parking garage located beneath the hotel, with access to our room by elevator. No carrying luggage upstairs here.

The first thing Wendy did, when we were settled into our room, was to take a shower, and the first thing I did was to open a cold beer from the mini-bar. After I had my turn at the shower, I was eager to venture out of the hotel for a ground-level look at the city. Life was good again.

A large two-story shopping mall adjoined the hotel, but we were more interested in the nearby place de la Comédie, which the hotel clerk had marked as being a particularly good area for finding a restaurant. It was a large plaza, with an ornate fountain at one end and an equally ornate opera house at the other. Both sides were lined with shops and several heavily patronized cafés whose tables extended far out into the square. On the fringe of one of the cafés, a magician had attracted a large crowd by performing a fire-eating act. Although the sun was now low in the sky, the temperature was still in the mid-eighties, rendering his act even more heroic.

There were tables available within the cafés, but the heat made them untenable. We walked with increasing hunger from one place to the next, despairing in the knowledge that when a table is taken, it may be held by the patron for the rest of the evening. Finally, resigned to the prospects of a supper consisting of the remains of our picnic lunch, we made our way back to the upper deck of the mall leading to our hotel. At least we could eat in the cool comfort of our room.

"One more time around the square," Wendy insisted.

"I thought you were tired."

"I am, but the crowd helps keep me from thinking about those poor, old people in Vence. It's been with me all day—all I could think of was what it must be like, being wheeled out each morning to face that graveyard." She shook her head as if trying once again to dislodge the thought. "You know that bumper sticker that says 'Today is the first day of the rest of your life'? The terrible thing is, I keep twisting it around and coming up with 'Today is the first day of the end of your life.'"

Her obvious distress must have caught the sympathetic eyes of a young couple sitting at a large table nearby. The girl made a sweeping motion with her hand, beckoning to us, and I heard that loveliest of all French words, *partage*—to share.

With one mind, unconcerned by what the menu might offer, we altered our course. After shrugging off our enthusiastic thank-you's while they made room at the table, the young couple seemed to lose interest in us. We feasted there on roast chicken and *frites*, with the lively sound of the square's milling crowd providing background music. The young couple sipped their wine and said little, touching hands occasionally and seeming content just to gaze at one another.

Wendy reached across the table and rested her hand gently on my arm, and neither of us marked the passing of the sun.

~ On Your Own ~

Vence

Although Vence is often seen in motion pictures (particularly the large urn of the Vieille Fontaine), the town is often overlooked by visitors in their rush to get to its more spectacularly situated neighbor, St.-Paul-de-Vence. Those with an artistic eye, however, have often found Vence the more attractive place to spend their time. The chapel of Matisse is well known, but less well advertised is the mosaic by Marc Chagall in the cathedral. Other artists and writers who have lived in the town include Dufy, André Gide, and D.H. Lawrence.

Attractions

Follow the signs to the tourist office and you will be in sight of the stubby tower and gate of the wall surrounding the **Vieille Ville** (old town). A walk along the wall will provide some fantastic views, but the real charm is in the narrow, cobbled streets and ancient houses.

Although the Romanesque **cathédrale** dates from the 10th century in its foundation, changes to the structure over the years have left it looking squat and gloomy, as though designed by committee. The interior seems cramped and dark, and even the Chagall mosaic fails to brighten it much.

The **Chapelle du Rosaire**, familiarly known as the **Matisse Chapel**, lies down a dusty stretch of road (ave. Henri-Matisse) which ultimately becomes route D2210 leading to the hill town of St-Jeannet. Phone: 93-58-03-25.

In the surrounding area:

Vence is the largest in a group of ancient hilltop towns in various stages of neglect or restoration. **St.-Paul-de-Vence**, about three miles southeast of Vence, is almost completely rebuilt and shines with a cleanliness never seen in medieval times, while **Coursegoules**, about ten miles north of Vence, still carries the dusty covering of the centuries.

A **circular drive**, providing a variety of visual treats and innumerable sites for picnicking, begins at Vence on route D2 to Coursegoules. About five miles past the town, turn left onto route D3, through the **gorges of the Loup**, and into **Le Bar**. From Le Bar, take route D2210 back to Vence. The entire excursion covers about sixty miles, so take your time and enjoy it.

The glitz of the **French Riviera** is only fifteen miles to the south on route D236. This road takes you to **Nice** by way of **Cagnes-sur-Mer-Villeneuve-Loubet**, a town notable for its racetrack, aptly named "le Hippodrome de la Côte d'Azur."

Hotels

The three small (10-12 rooms) hotels listed below all have excellent restaurants and offer demi-pensions (breakfast and dinner) at bargain rates.

The **Auberge des Seigneurs** (at place du Friêne, near the tourist office in Vence) has been around to serve travelers for over four centuries, and it is easy to imagine that you have been magically transported back in time when you first step into the Great Hall with its open fireplace and rows of hanging copper pots. The accommodations have been updated to include a shower in every room. Closed from October 15 to December 1. Rates: 300-320F ($60-64), with free parking. The restaurant features open-hearth roasting and grilling; menus: 200-230F ($40-46). Phone: 93-58-04-24.

The **Closerie des Genêts** (4, impasse M. Maurel, Vence) has been recently upgraded to include showers in all rooms. The flowers in the courtyard and the furnishings within create the feel of a country home rather than an inn—it's our favorite place to stop in the area. Closed November 10 to December 20. Rates: 300-340F ($60-68), with free parking. The restaurant features country cooking at its best; menus: 140-180F ($28-36). Phone: 93-58-33-25.

La Roseraie (route de Coursegoules—follow ave. Henri-Giraud out of Vence to route D2) is a converted 19th-century manor house surrounded by a lovely garden, providing some of its rooms with private terraces. On warm nights, the terrace of the restaurant is set up for candlelight dining. Closed all of January. Rates: 390F ($78), with free parking. The restaurant features recipes from the Dordogne and Aquitaine regions; menus: 180-200F ($36-40). Phone: 93-58-02-20.

The Côte d'Azur: Fréjus

The fast-paced péage A8/E80 bypasses countless small fishing villages along the Mediterranean coast, some famous and others as yet unspoiled by notoriety. Just southwest of Cannes, you can exit the péage onto route N98, leading you to Fréjus, originally a Roman naval base. Following its destruction by the Saracens in 940, the city was rebuilt behind a new fortified wall and provided with a new cathedral which was completed around 1200.

Attractions

Some remnants of the early Roman settlement still remain: the **amphitheatre**, an **arena** still in use today for bull fights and rock concerts, **a theatre** now used for summer shows, a few arches of an **aqueduct**, some small baths, and an occasional pillar incorporated into a medieval building.

The **Musée Archéologique** has the usual displays of pots, amphorae, and lamps, but in addition, has a beautifully complete Roman mosaic depicting leopards.

For those with a taste for the more modern, the **Foundation Daniel Templon** displays the post-1945 works of French artists.

In the surrounding area:

Driving further down N98, you pass through **Ste.-Maxime** across the bay from **St.-Tropez**. A stop at either town will leave blisters on your wallet as your money streams out at explosive speed. For a more delightful drive, turn onto route D559 toward **Le Lavandou**. Relatively unspoiled fishing villages dot the coast along the **Baie de Cavataire**, and hotels are plentiful in **La Croix-Valmer** and **Cavalaire-sur-Mer** (not to be confused with the ideally picturesque Cavaliere which lies further down the coast). If you are traveling during the off-season of the year (October-April), you should have little trouble in obtaining rooms at a reasonable (never cheap) price.

Hotels

Resort towns at the beach are not generally places to look for inexpensive hotels. However, both listed here offer clean, comfortable rooms at reasonable rates.

Auberge du Vieux Four (49, rue Grisolle, Fréjus) is located in the old town near the cathedral, maintaining the rustic appearance of an old inn. An excellent restaurant is attached. Closed from September 20 to October 20 and all of February. Rates: 250-330F ($50-66). Phone: 94-51-56-38.

L'Oasis (rue Fabre-ave. Hippolyte, Fréjus) has no restaurant, but the location, 3 blocks from the beach, makes it popular. Closed February and November. Rates: 300-450F ($60-90). Phone: 94-51-50-44.

Restaurants

The restaurant at **Le Vieux Four** (49, rue Grisolle, Fréjus) is sure to please, even if you were unable to stay in the hotel. Menus: 200 to 350F ($40-70). Phone: 94-51-56-38.

Les Potiers (135, rue Potiers, Fréjus) offers special dishes based upon seasonal availability. This is the place to go for a lighter taste of French cuisine. Menus: 125-250F ($25-50). Phone: 94-51-33-74.

The Côte d'Azur: Toulon

*Beyond le Lavandou, N98 joins the péage A57 into the naval port of Toulon, one of the finest natural harbors in the world and in continuous use since the days of the Romans. Heavily bombed during World War II, the rebuilding was done under the direction of the military with predictable results. Fortunately, much of the **Vieille Ville** (old town) was spared and there is much to see within the area extending from the old port and blvd. de Strasbourg. One of the features that is particularly striking here is the number of fountains—most featuring dolphins.*

Attractions

The markets of the **Poissonerie** and the **Marché** (near cours Lafayette) are both fun to see in the early morning hours.

A find for fans of medieval history, the earliest portions of the grand **Cathédrale de Ste.-Marie-Majeure** date from the 11th and 12th centuries.

The **Arsenal Maritime** sports an entrance of monumental proportions—it looks Greek, but was built in 1738.

The **Grosse Tour de la Mître**, with its surrounding moat, was constructed by an Italian in 1514 for Louis XII. Today, it houses a small maritime museum within the seven pillboxes at its base. Among the exhibits is a piece of elaborately decorated artillery from China. Admission: 12F ($2.40).

A larger exhibit of maritime history and paraphernalia can be seen at the **Musée de la Marine** (place Monsenergue). Admission: 22F ($4.40). Phone: 94-02-02-01.

If the French Navy is in port, a fantastic view can be had from **Mount Faron**. Drive along the corniche du Mont-Faron on the lower slopes, or take the funicular from blvd. Amiral-Vence to the top for 30F ($6). Very impressive at sunset, with the slanting shadows turning the city into a vast bas-relief and, in the distance, the blue Mediterranean absorbing the light to become Homer's wine dark sea. Caution: the funicular stops running at 6:00 pm.

In the surrounding area:

Some of the most spectacular views lie between Toulon and Marseille, from the fishing villages of **Sanary, Bandol, Les Lecques,** and the yacht-harbor town of **Cassis** to the sheer escarpments between **La Ciotat** and **Cassis**. The road clings to the top of cliffs which plunge fifteen hundred feet or more down to the sea. Take route D559 out of Toulon, or take the *péage* A50 and turn onto D559 at Bandol.

Hotels

La Corniche (1, Littoral Frédéric-Mistral, Toulon) lies in the more sedate quarter of Le Mourillon, sporting a woodsy decor with real ivy growing on real trees in the dining room. To get there, drive out to where a point of land, capped by the Tour Royale, juts out into the Mediterranean. Rates: 490-510F ($98-102), and parking 40F ($8). Phone: 94-41-35-12.

Toulon is the home port for the French Navy, and the following hotels, although beyond reproach, are located in the old town which tends to be boisterous and bawdy at night. Near the waterfront, only "working girls" walk the streets at night without an escort.

Le Jaurès (11, rue Jean Jaurès) is located away from the waterfront. No restaurant. Rates: 200-250F ($40-50). Phone: 94-92-83-04.

Maritima (9, rue Gimelli), near the train station, also has no restaurant. Rates: 175-275F ($35-55). Phone: 94-92-39-33.

Restaurants

Toulon is well supplied with brasseries and cafés, all ready to serve fresh seafood in addition to the standard fare.

For substantial meal, try **La Madeleine** (7, rue des Tombades, near the cathedral), which features the cuisine of Provence. Menus: 100-170F ($20-35). Closed Tuesdays and Wednesdays. Phone: 94-92-67-85.

La Ferme (6, place Louis-Blanc) is decorated in a rustic style, but its cuisine is moderne. Only the freshest ingredients are used, and it is well worth the few extra francs you will pay. Menus: 130-225F ($26-45). Closed Sundays and all of August. Phone: 94-41-43-74.

Marseille

Marseille has the reputation of being a rough city, and this reputation, unfortunately, has discouraged many tourists from visiting this dynamic sea port. Over centuries of wars and revolutions, Marseille has remained the principal center of trade on the Mediterranean, borrowing from all cultures to form a truly cosmopolitan city. A fascinating afternoon may be spent at a sidewalk café doing nothing other than watching and listening to the multicolored and multilingual passersby.

Attractions

The **Château d'If** can be reached by a 20-minute boat ride for 40F ($8) round trip. Admission to the château is included in the fare. Catch the boat in the Vieux-Port (old port) at the quai des Belges. Phone: 91-59-02-30.

The **Palais Longchamp** (at place Bernex at the end of blvd. Longchamp) houses the **Musée des Beaux-Arts**. The palace was built in the 19th century during the Second Empire and reflects the grandeur of the period that saw the reconstruction of Paris under Napoleon II. The works of Honoré Daumier, the French caricaturist (born in Marseille in 1908), rate some time if you can spare it from viewing the vast assortment of paintings from the 16th through 19th centuries, including works by Rubens, Corot, Courbet, Millet, David, and Monticelli. An extra attraction is the salon devoted to the sculpture of Pierre Puget. Admission 12F ($2.40). Phone: 91-62-21-17.

The **Basilique de Notre-Dame-de-la-Garde** is of interest mainly because of its location on the heights above the Vieux-Port. The building itself was built in the 19th century in a mixture of Romanesque and quasi-Oriental architecture that serves neither style well. You can drive or take a bus from the Vieux-Port to a parking lot 600 feet below the basilica, but you must walk the remaining distance—all uphill. Both the view and the climb are breathtaking.

The **Ancienne Cathédrale de la Major** is a 12th-century church which borrowed its architecture from the Byzantine, capping its roofs with bulbous domes, while the rest of Europe was raising Gothic spires.

Hotels

Grand Hôtel Genève-Vieux-Port (3 bis, rue Reine-Elisabeth) provides excellent views of the port from the most expensive rooms. Public parking is nearby. No restaurant. Rates: 350-500F ($70-100). Phone: 91-90-51-42.

La Residence du Vieux-Port (18, quai du Port) is a centrally located hotel, nicely decorated with baroque sculpture and antiques, with a café for light meals. Rates: 325-450F ($65-90), and parking 50F ($10). Phone: 91-91-91-22.

Restaurants

There are plenty of *brasseries* and cafés on la Canebière and around the Vieux-Port. For a touch of Paris, try the one called **Brasserie New-York Vieux Port** (7, quai Belges). Phone: 91-33-60-98.

Two restaurants, each of which rates a star from Michelin, specialize in bouillabaisse and are located within casting distance of each other. The one you choose may depend upon how your schedule fits with their vacation closings. **Restaurant Calypso** (3, rue des Catalans) is closed Sundays, Mondays, and all of August. Menus: 250-400F ($40-80). Phone: 91-52-64-00. **Restaurant Michel** (6, rue des Catalans) is closed Tuesdays, Wednesdays, and all of July. Menus: 270-450F ($54-90). Phone: 91-52-30-63.

Along the rue des Trois-Rois are several restaurants, each with a distinct personality. My favorite was the **Le King Restaurant** (12, rue des Trois-Rois), dedicated to the memory of Elvis Presley. The costumed *maître d'hotel* bore a striking resemblance to "The King" himself. Menus: 150-275F ($30-55). Phone: 91-42-88-47.

Wendy favored **Le Balthazar** (8, rue des Trois-Rois) for its chic, strictly French atmosphere. I didn't mind the low prices for both food and wine. Menus: 85-150F ($17-30). No reservations.

Chapter 7

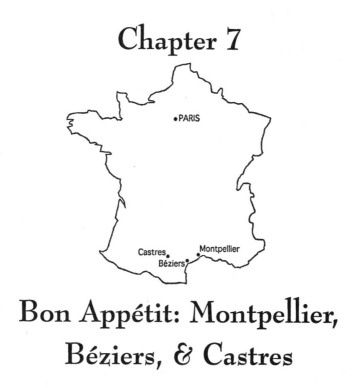

Bon Appétit: Montpellier, Béziers, & Castres

The next morning we awoke with energy restored from our night's sleep in the cool, air-conditioned room. We decided to skip the breakfast offered by the hotel, at the fixed price of $12 apiece, and take our chances at one of the sidewalk cafés in the place de la Comédie. When we checked out, the desk clerk graciously offered us the day's use of the parking garage, allowing us to explore the city without worrying about the car—a further justification for the extravagance of staying at a luxury hotel.

The sky was clear, and the sun already promised another sweltering day, even at eight in the morning. We retraced our path to the previous evening's café and found a table with a good view of the plaza, alive with scurrying people on their way to work. Some hurried by, without a glance at the café; others would wave and shout "*Ça va*," to acquaintances or occasionally stop for a ritualistic handshake or triple-kiss on the cheeks.

The deftness and rapidity with which the triple-kiss is exchanged has always been a source of amazement to us, for we have never seen a missed cue. Simultaneously, both parties turn their heads slightly to the right, touch cheeks, and kiss the air before withdrawing in order to quickly shift the set of their heads to the left. Cheeks are again brushed, the air kissed, and heads returned to the right, where the original maneuver is repeated. All is done in the blink of an eye, with never a mistake. It must be that the French have an inborn sense of right and left; otherwise, the dental offices would be overwhelmed by casualties.

Over breakfast, we studied the little map the hotel clerk had provided, trying to get a feel for the layout of the city. Like most European cities, Montpellier developed in the form of concentric circles; as the population grew, new buildings would be built next to the walls of the old city, and main streets would be extended through the gates of the city walls like spokes on a wheel. Secondary streets that did not lead to a gate would end at the peripheral road, requiring a pedestrian to turn right or left, until he reached one of the main roads. (This was the pattern used by Pierre L'Enfant in the city plan for Washington, D.C.) Beautiful as the design may be in the abstract, it can be quite baffling to the tourist who takes a wrong turn or assumes that streets run in parallel lines.

We walked across the plaza to an adjoining open space, the Esplanade, a long parkway with its center divider planted in contrasting mounds of impatiens under large plane trees. Halfway down the walk, the area on the right opened to reveal an expanse of grass surrounding a serene pond, its surface disturbed only by a mother duck and three little puff-ball ducklings trailing single-file in her wake. We stopped for a moment, marveling at the ability of the French to create such areas of quietude within the noisiest business districts of their cities.

Leaving the Esplanade, we boldly approached the old city on a road which our map showed leading directly to the Promenade du Peyrou, famed for its water temple and aqueduct. We were tempted to stop at the Musée Fabre, which boasts some fabulous paintings by David, Ingres, Gericault, Delacroix, and Courbet, but it was a Monet morning, and we were loath to waste it within the confines of a museum which specialized in the academicians, no matter how grand the exhibition.

We knew that we had entered the old city by the narrowing of the road and the signs that prohibited automobiles. The sidewalks had become narrow ledges, designed to allow an escape for pedestrians from the wheels of a carriage, or more likely, to prevent carriage wheels from grinding into the walls of the buildings.

The road did not run straight, as depicted on the map, and we were forced to choose between going right or left almost immediately. To the right, we could see where another narrow street intersected; to the left, the road curved into the unknown. We took the path to the right and turned the corner, heading deeper into the old city. It was very still, and we found the absence of automobile traffic somewhat disquieting. It was as though some divine hand had abolished the 20th century with a wave. We saw only one car, when a crack in one of the many massive gates allowed us to peek into a courtyard at an ancient Citroen on blocks, looking as though it had been made of corrugated roofing tin and old canvas. A black-and-white cat glared suspiciously from under it as we walked by. The buildings seemed to close in on us, and the air felt moist and heavy, still there was no sign of the broad avenue we had been promised by the map. "I think we had better go back. This doesn't look right," I said, thinking that we would really become lost if we continued.

"Yes, I don't like this," Wendy agreed. We had taken only a few steps back, when a high-pitched voice called from across the street.

"*Madame, monsieur! Bonjour. Vous êtes étrangers?*" A woman was calling from a secondary doorway, one cut into the corner of a larger carriage door. There was no way of telling how long she may have watched our uncertain ramblings.

"*Bonjour, madame,*" I replied. "*Nous sommes perdus.*" I admitted that we were lost.

"*Ah, Américains,*" she exclaimed, arm outstretched and palm upturned in the universal signal to stop. "*Restez un moment.*"

"How did she know that we're Americans?" I whispered.

"Your accent," Wendy answered.

"But I only said a couple of words."

The slight woman opened the door wide and stepped over the high sill, allowing us only a momentary glimpse of the garden courtyard on the other side before she closed the door. She was dressed in a white blouse and flowered skirt and had lightly flung a colorful scarf over her head. Her round, brown eyes made a perfect match for her round face, and the corners of her small mouth were turned up in a smile as she asked, "Where do you wish to go?" Her accent was definitely British.

Dumbly, I held out the map and then answered, "We were going to see the water temple."

"Ah, Le Château d'Eau. Come, I will show you." She headed back the way we had first come. "Will you stay in Montpellier for long?" she asked over her shoulder, as she forged ahead with a speed unexpected from one so tiny.

"Only today," Wendy joined in. "It's really nice of you to go out of your way like this."

"*Pas de quoi,*" she replied, making light of her effort. "It is too bad that you are staying such a short time. Montpellier, it is a beautiful city."

We passed the street that led back to the museum, the intersection where I had made the wrong turn, and followed our guide around the curve in the road to the next intersection. She waited until we had drawn abreast, then, as though presenting us with a precious jewel, indicated with a sweep of her arm, "*Voilà, Le Château d'Eau.*"

We looked down the broad, straight avenue to its terminus at the steps of a marble temple that might well have been transported from some Greek isle. On a small scale, it was like looking down the Champs-Élysèes to the Arc de Triomphe in Paris.

"It is beautiful," Wendy said. "Thank you for showing us. Would you join us for some coffee or tea?"

"Non," she replied. "I must go. I have many things to do. *Au revoir, mes amis.* Enjoy my city."

"Thank you again," I called after her, but she never looked back. "Should I have offered her money?" I asked Wendy.

"She would have been insulted. Didn't you notice her clothes?"

"Yeah, they looked nice and cool. Just right for this climate."

"Very expensive." Wendy explained. "Ferragamo shoes. Hermès scarf—not your everyday housewife."

We meandered down the rue Foch, looking in the shop windows, admiring the well-kept homes that lined the side streets, feeling at ease once again, with a destination clearly in sight. The promenade du Peyrou is a large, rectangular plaza, twice the size of the place de la Comédie, with a large equestrian statue of Louis XIV dominating the highest level, an obvious expression of political correctness, since the construction of the promenade was begun in 1688.

Standing next to the statue, the sweep of the view was truly magnificent. To the north, we could see for miles, across a patchwork quilt of vineyards and sunflower fields, all the way to the craggy mountains on the horizon. To the south, the flatter land was marked by numerous small lakes that reflected the blue of the sky. On a clear day, one could probably see the Mediterranean; unfortunately, a summer haze blurred our vision, and we could barely discern the outlines of a couple coastal villages.

We found each of Le Château d'Eau's five sides to be comprised of an ornate arch, framed by two Corinthian columns supporting the unadorned cornices. Roofless, the light reaches down into the tiled cistern which is filled with rushing water from the arched aqueduct to the west. Flanked by two stairways, the design is one of perfect symmetry and proportion, classic in inspiration and restrained in execution.

The area behind the temple was wide enough that, by walking to either corner of the plaza, we could easily see the aqueduct. Unlike the temple, which reflected a Grecian influence, the aqueduct was pure Roman. A double tier of arches stretched for almost a half mile, straight as an arrow to the west. The wide arcades of the lower tier were about double the sizes of those they supported, giving the whole a feeling of great stability. Although it lacked the towering height, and had only two tiers, it looked like a replica of the Pont du Gard near Nîmes.

By noon, the heat was becoming oppressive, and having seen enough, we started back to pick up the car at the hotel. At the place de la Comédie, people were crowded around the sidewalk café, waiting for tables. Although a cold sandwich, made from a foot-long piece of baguette filled with tender country ham, and a cold beer were appealing, the prospect of waiting in the hot sun was a compelling argument against prolonging our stay. We picked up our car, feeling that Montpellier truly deserved more attention and warranted a return visit—some day in October when the weather was cooler.

Once free of the city, the heat became less oppressive as with windows open we rolled past miles of tidy vineyards, interspersed with orchards of plums and peaches. Seeing all the fruit hanging heavy on the trees served as a constant reminder that we had foregone lunch.

While the *péage* is a fast and direct road to Béziers, it is admittedly lacking in anything interesting to see along the way. As we made the drive this time, perhaps to distract ourselves from our growing hunger, we reminisced of a prior, more leisurely tour we had taken through the area. On that occasion we made a short backtrack, traveling across a memorable stretch of swamp, sand and salt-grass, to the historic city of Aigues-Mortes.

We found the stone walls of the Tour de Constance, the central tower of Aigues-Mortes' medieval battlements, standing as they were placed by the troops of Louis IX, built in the late 13th century to protect the port of embarkation of the Seventh Crusade. We climbed the northwest corner of the tower in the early morning, when the mists were still swirling over the marshes like the ghosts of centuries past.

Outside the walls, we were treated to an impromptu bull fight, where victory was claimed, not through the death of the bull, but by plucking a flower from his horns as he charged by. Inside the walls, everything was arranged to separate the tourist from his money—confirming the legend that if all the splinters of the True Cross sold to the crusaders in Aigues-Mortes were to be connected, the bridge made would reach Béziers.

This day, however, the only swampy, medieval tower we saw was in our minds, and after an hour or so we reached lovely Béziers. We drove down the allée Paul-Riquet, a broad avenue that stretches from the theatre on place de la Victoire to the Plateau des Poètes and which, like the Champs-Élysées in Paris, provides a focus for life in the city. Shaded by innumerable trees, it's a street seemingly designed to please the eye, rather than to facilitate the flow of traffic.

Parking was permitted on both sides of the central dividing strip, where enterprising restaurants had established outposts. Banks of umbrella-shaded tables were served from restaurants across the street, requiring the waiters to make a perilous passage from kitchen to table through street traffic. We found a parking place near one of the parkway restaurants and quickly established ourselves at a table.

We were soon discovered by a waiter who, with a long face, explained that the special of the day, lasagna, had already been consumed by those who had arrived on time. However, he continued, the moussaka with leeks was still available and even more delicious. The bewildering thought of eating a Greek specialty in a French restaurant because they had run out of an Italian dish brought into focus how meaningless national borders have been in the culture of the Mediterranean. Having received food for both thought and sustenance, we again resumed our journey.

A few miles out of Béziers, we abruptly left the flatlands and began climbing into the rocky hills to the north. The vineyards grew smaller and began to be supplanted by sunflowers, and the fruit trees disappeared, except for scattered clusters near solitary farmhouses. Curious rock formations thrust above the low buttes that encircled the broad plain. Outlined against the sky, they assumed the shapes of castles, church spires, or gigantic animals and birds. Closer and closer we approached, until, quite suddenly, we were in a mountain pass, with those rocky crags hovering above. It was easy to imagine that this was the haunt of stags and the ferocious *sanglier*, the wild boar, and although we saw no sign of either, it seemed the perfect setting for the fairy tale, "Beauty and the Beast."

A short time later, we were out of the pass and on another broad plain of sunflowers which seemed to extend for miles. A single sunflower in bloom may be of passing interest, more for its ungainly construction than for its questionable beauty. Viewed alone, it is a ragtag scarecrow of a plant; when seen en masse, however, the individual plant is lost in the glittering and shimmering of the whole golden field.

Our first view of Castres was suitable for framing. A small flock of sheep were clustered near the crest of the hill that swept gracefully down to the River Agout. Stretching along both sides of the river, the pale ocher walls and red-tiled roofs of the city glowed in the afternoon sun. Three ancient stone bridges connected the divided city with looping, symmetrical arches, while a fourth bridge of steel and concrete stood in sorry isolation downstream. The highway carried us over the modern bridge, affording a closer view of the old bridges and the concrete weir that stretched across the river, backing up the water so it was as calm as a reflecting pool.

Once in the city, we drove parallel to the river, expecting to see the usual sign directing us to the tourist office. Traffic was light in the heat of the afternoon, so we easily found a parking space overlooking the river and near a sidewalk café that offered an even better view. Since the drive from Béziers had taken less than an hour, we had plenty of time to settle back with a cold beer and enjoy the reflections of the colorful buildings across the placid water.

Rising three and four stories above the water's edge, the structures looked to be quite old, but the loving care of their occupants was evident in the bright paint on their facades. Shuttered windows were embellished with window-boxes of bright red geraniums, and one particularly impressive unit sported three tiers of wrought-iron balconies, each supporting rows of potted impatiens.

The quiet of the scene was broken by the arrival of a launch that drifted down from upstream. After the passengers had disembarked, one of the crew carried a large wooden signboard up to the foot of the bridge and carefully placed it so that it would be seen by anyone interested in a boat ride. This invitation did not go unnoticed by Wendy and me, but for the moment we were loath to move from our chairs.

It was so tranquil; it seemed unbelievable that we could be in the heart of the Huguenot lands that time and again had witnessed such barbaric slaughter. In the 13th century, Béziers was ravaged during the Albigensian crusade, and 15,000 men, women, and children fell to the swords of northern knights. In the 16th and 17th centuries, Henry IV revoked the freedom of religion granted under his Edict of Nantes and mercilessly expanded his rule into the lands of Provence and Toulouse, slaughtering thousands more Protestant Huguenots. It is no wonder that a heritage of hatred and mistrust of Parisian officialdom still bubbles beneath the surface of this population.

"It's so beautiful and peaceful here," Wendy said. "Why don't we spend the night here and go on to Albi tomorrow?"

"And maybe take a cruise on the river later?" I responded.

"Why not?"

So it was decided. I dug out the red *Michelin Guide* to see what hotels were available in Castres; while lacking the personality of a tourist office, this is still our most valuable guide, with a reliable map for every major town in France. We had located our choice, the Grand Hôtel, before finishing our beers. The hotel, just two blocks from where we had parked, was built with a view of the river and, although its grandness had faded somewhat, was neat and clean.

After checking in, we took a few minutes to explore the nearby Jardins du Palais Episcopal, a beautiful formal garden, reminiscent of those at the Château de Villandry, with boxwood hedges clipped and trimmed into intricate geometric patterns. Banks of brilliant cannas raised their flowering spikes of red, yellow, and orange along the perimeter, giving a flamboyant relief to the austere formality of the garden.

Not being one to sit for long when adventure beckons, it was Wendy's turn to suggest the boat ride. "Why not?" I said, echoing her earlier comment, and we set off to see the sights from the decks of the river barge.

The boat was an exact replica, with the exception of the large windows in the cabin, of the flat-bottomed river boats that carried cargo up and down the Agout in the 19th century. It was wide of beam and very stable. The wood was varnished to a sheen that would make a yachtsman envious. Banks of benches lined the interior of the cabin, providing room for the passengers to sit three abreast, like the oarsmen on a Roman galley. The boat filled with passengers quickly, and soon we were on our way upriver, past the riverside apartment buildings and into the country. Here the dwellings were fewer, but more elegant, with beautiful gardens and well-kept lawns that sloped down to the water's edge. A small boy lifted one hand from his fishing rod to wave as we surged by, but otherwise we saw no sign of the people who lived on those country estates.

After a half-hour, the boat pulled up to a wooden dock and all of the passengers began to disembark. Only then did we realize that we had booked passage, not on a river cruise, but on a water taxi filled with commuters.

Returning to Castres, we discovered that due to the Grand Hôtel's need to cut expenses (by eliminating the restaurant staff!) there would be no dinner served at our hotel that night. Checking the Michelin, we found two restaurants. We quickly eliminated the first from consideration because it would entail driving about five miles out of town, and the drive back in the dark after a full dinner and a bottle of wine was out of the question. The second listing seemed promising and was located within a few blocks of the hotel.

We set out in high spirits, admiring the sunset across the river as we walked, ready for a new adventure in dining. We turned and followed a cross-street a block away from the river, only to find our chosen restaurant closed, with a sign indicating that it would remain so throughout the entire month of August. We felt betrayed. How could they take an entire month for vacation when we were hungry?

Once again we were forced to depend upon the good offices of the native population for help. An approaching gentleman, wearing a suit and vest despite the heat, looked as though he would know good food. I left Wendy, still studying the sign in disbelief, and stepped forward. "*Pardonnez moi, monsieur.*"

He stopped, fixing me with a glare that threatened physical violence should the need arise, but I pressed on, using the phrase so carefully memorized in French class, "*Où se trouve un bon restaurant, près d'ici?*"

His glare was replaced by a slight smile, as though in relief at not being asked for a handout. He was quick to respond. "*Là-bas,*" he gestured toward the bridge. "*La rive gauche.*"

I uttered a grateful "*Merci, monsieur,*" and hurried back to Wendy with the good news. "We eat tonight!"

"Where?"

"He said, 'Over there, on the left bank.'"

We crossed the bridge, past the dock where the water taxi was tied up for the night, and turned right at the first street that seemed to parallel the river. We were rewarded almost immediately by the sight of a restaurant that proudly featured pizza. I was dumbfounded. "This can't be it!"

"Are you sure this is the left bank?" Wendy questioned. "If you're looking upstream, it would be the right bank."

I had never given the question any serious thought before, just blindly accepted the label as it applied to Paris without considering whether I was looking up or down the Seine.

"Let's go on," Wendy added. "If we don't find anything better, we can always come back."

The road we now walked down was paved with macadam, that uncharming black mix of tar and crushed rock that had become the symbol for the modernization of France, replacing the more artistic, ankle-twisting cobbles on its streets. The buildings on either side looked old in the way they look in the older parts of U.S. cities, dingy and starting to crumble, but lacking the patina and charm of the truly old. There was no hint of the beautiful exteriors these same buildings exhibited on their riverfront sides. "We're on the side where they collect garbage," Wendy said with conviction. Although there were no garbage cans in evidence, her words summarized our feeling that we were walking in an area not meant for public display.

The next block looked a bit more promising for, while the backsides of the waterfront properties were still drab, those across the street had endeavored to be presentable. Midway down, the pale glow of neon beckoned with the promise of some commercial activity, and we hurried toward it. A large curved arch of brown stone had been artfully set into the facade of the building, giving the effect of a medieval cloister. Centered behind a plate-glass window within the arch, a small neon sign spelled out "La Rive Gauche."

"Look, 'the Left Bank,'" Wendy cried. "We've found it."

"Well, what do *you* know? The man didn't say that was the name of the restaurant."

"Who cares? We can eat!" she exclaimed with feeling. Then as we looked through the window, her tone changed to concern. "It looks deserted. Are we too early?"

I checked my watch. "Seven-thirty. Maybe a little early, but we'd better go in while there are still tables."

Inside, we were greeted by a man in a dark business suit. *"Bonsoir madame, monsieur. Vous desirez le dîner?"*

"Oui, monsieur. Dîner pour deux, s'il vous plaît," I answered gamely.

"Bien. Par ici," he said, leading the way past tables set with glistening silver and crystal atop mauve tablecloths that matched the muted floral wallpaper. Each table had a lighted candle in a crystal chimney beside a bud vase with a single rose and a spray of fern. The soft lighting from the polished-brass chandelier hanging from the beamed ceiling cast a glow that promised an evening of elegant dining.

We were seated at a table for two, and as our host lifted a napkin from Wendy's plate and lowered it to her lap with a sweeping gesture, he asked us in English, "Would you care for an aperitif?"

Wendy gave him a look of gratitude and answered, "A glass of white wine would be nice." He turned toward me, with his eyebrows raised in question.

"Two glasses of Muscadet or Sancerre. Whatever you have open will do."

He returned in a moment with two glasses and menus. "We had a nice Sancerre opened," he said as he placed the glasses before us and the menus on the table at one side. "Please call when you are ready to order." He left us, returning to the front, ready for the arrival of the next guests.

The menu offered three fixed-price dinners, each with a choice of entrée along with hors d'oeuvre, soup, salad and dessert. The price of each dinner was determined by the number of courses desired, and since the dinner was to be the evening's entertainment, it seemed appropriate to be a little more lavish

than usual. "I don't think that I can handle a seven-course dinner," I said, "but the 150-franc looks like a bargain."

"How much is that?" Wendy asked.

"About thirty dollars."

"Okay, you order for me. Just no fish soup."

I signaled to the man in front, and he left his lonely vigil to
hurry toward us, notebook in hand. "We'll both have the 150
menu," I said. "We'd like to start with the melon. What is the
soup tonight?"

"We have a nice bouillabaisse . . ."

Wendy's antennae vibrated.

"Or a country vegetable."

"Country vegetable for both," I said and Wendy relaxed.

"And the fish course?" he asked. "We have a salmon mousse,
or filet of sole almondine."

"Filet of sole," we said in unison.

"For the entrée, may I suggest the lamb? It is perfect, a specialty of the region." He spoke with such authority that we knew
it would be a mistake to order anything different. The salad and
dessert would be chosen later, but the wine choice could not wait.
From the wine list, I chose a moderately priced bottle of red
Cahors. He looked surprised by my selection. "You are English,
then?"

"No, we're American."

"I thought only the English knew the wines of Cahors.
Americans usually order a Burgundy or Bordeaux."

"Cahors is half the price and just as good," I responded.

"Perhaps it is better." He smiled, as though sharing a confidence, before he folded his notepad and headed toward the
kitchen at the back of the restaurant.

A moment later, a young man wearing the black tie and vest
of a French waiter came out of the kitchen, bearing a tray from
which he carefully removed a plate of sliced baguette and two

tubs of butter. Then, wonder of wonders, he produced two large glasses of water which tinkled with cracked ice. Like most Americans traveling abroad, we had long ago gotten used to the fact that it is quite rare in Europe to receive water without specifically requesting it. *"Bon appétit,"* he said and hurried back to the kitchen.

"Who says the French don't like Americans?" Wendy said as she toasted the restaurant with upraised water glass.

"The same people who say that the waiters are rude," I responded.

We hardly had a chance to sample the water before the waiter returned with our hors d'oeuvres. He placed a picture-perfect plate before each. We had expected the standard chilled whole melon on crushed ice, but were delighted instead to see slices of peeled melon, arranged in a pinwheel pattern, between artfully centered florets of pink, paper-thin slices of dry-cured Bayonne ham (France's answer to the prosciutto of Parma). Wedges of fresh lime completed the presentation, adding just the right contrast of color.

"It's almost too pretty to eat," Wendy said.

"Never!" I exclaimed as I placed a bit of ham upon a piece of melon. "Pretty is as pretty tastes." The ham, sweet and smooth as velvet provided the perfect complement to the musky melon. With my full concentration on the melon and ham, I had not noticed the restaurateur desert his vigil at the front to deliver the bottle of Cahors we had ordered.

The long cork was worked free without a sound and a small splash poured into a goblet for my sampling. A quick swirl against the light from the candle revealed a clear, deep ruby color. A pass beneath the nose and I knew that we were about to enjoy a superb wine, for it smelled of cherries and cassis, with an earthy overlay that hinted at truffles and moist oak. I sipped and was amply rewarded.

"Excellent," I said, fighting off the desire to forego the remaining melon and concentrate on the wine. We still had half glasses of the Sancerre to see us through the soup and fish courses, but it had little appeal after having tasted the lovely Cahors.

The waiter next brought out the plates of soup at the precise moment we had finished the melon. A clear, steaming broth with thin slices of carrot and leek, it rapidly disappeared before the onslaught of our appetites, to be followed by plates of delicately browned Dover sole, glistening with butter beneath slivers of toasted almonds. Everything was done with such superb timing that I had to comment on it to Wendy.

"They have nothing else to do." She explained, "We're the only ones here." Since she was seated facing toward the front of the restaurant, she had been able to watch the man by the door as he interrupted his vigil to signal our waiter whenever service was required.

I turned to look at the empty restaurant, unable to believe that the availability of such good food and service had not attracted an overcapacity crowd. The expanse of empty tables stood invitingly, but there were no passersby in the street beyond. The man in front saw me turn, and he hurried back to ensure that all was right.

"Everything is perfect," Wendy replied.

I nodded my agreement before I interjected, in a tone intended to indicate my sympathy, "Is it a slow night for you?"

He shrugged his shoulders and said, "It happens." Then he filled our goblets with the Cahors and removed the empty white-wine glasses. "Your entrée should be ready. I will check."

"Is he trying to hurry us?" Wendy asked as she pushed the last bit of fish and crunchy almond onto her fork.

"I wouldn't blame him for wanting to close early, if we're his only customers." I finished the last of my sole and added, "If the food weren't so good, I'd feel guilty keeping them here."

The waiter now reappeared and removed the empty fish plates. He was quickly followed by the *maître d'hotel* who carried in a large platter with a crown roast of lamb surrounded by an assortment of vegetables. After the lamb was carved into separate chops and skillfully arranged before us on the plates, the juices from the platter (enhanced by thimble-sized morel mushrooms) were spooned over the meat, releasing a heavenly aroma of Provençal herbs. The two men stood, waiting for our reaction to the first taste.

Wendy was first. "It's lovely," she said. "No garlic. I think this is the first time that I ever really tasted lamb. All that I could taste before was the garlic."

I nodded my agreement as I savored my first bite. Hints of thyme and rosemary were tantalizingly mixed with the delicate, sweet flavor of young lamb, so different from the mutton that is often substituted. "Perfect," I said, wishing that I could think of some French phrase to adequately describe my pleasure. "Are you the owner of the restaurant?" I asked.

He nodded.

"It's really marvelous," I said, "the best food we've had since we left Paris. The *Michelin* people certainly slipped up by not listing you."

He raised his eyebrows in surprise. "But we are in the *Michelin*. Two forks."

Wendy looked questioningly at me and, with a slight smile, demurely asked, "When did we buy that guidebook?"

My mind raced back through the years, trying to pinpoint the date. "Let's see, must have been in 1985, maybe 1986."

"The world moves on," she said and smiled broadly.

Two plates of bright-green limestone lettuce were brought after we finished the lamb. I poked at it with my fork, wondering where I could find room for even a single bite. Wendy looked equally dispassionate, but gamely observed, "It's mostly water, you know. You can do it."

"I'll have to skip dessert," I replied and reluctantly began with the salad. It was delicious. Just the right touch of mustard in the vinaigrette brightened the taste buds so that each bite demanded another. I underwent a remarkable transformation. Whereas I had felt stuffed after the entrée, after finishing the salad I was again hungry enough to actually anticipate the cheese course with pleasure.

The waiter cleared the table and set a large platter of various cheeses in its center. Chèvre, brie, port salud, and roquefort, along with several balls of local country cheeses, made the selection most difficult. Although my mouth watered at the thought of such a bountiful supply, my tight belt reminded me that I had already overestimated my capacity. I settled for a small slice of the creamy, blue-veined roquefort, and Wendy had a slice of the well-ripened brie.

We were finishing the last of the Cahors when the waiter returned to ask about dessert. Wendy looked distressed. "I can't," she gasped.

"Just some fruit," I ordered. "Whatever you have will be fine."

Our host brought the dessert himself, slices of fresh peaches arranged in a pinwheel around scoops of peach sorbet. "From just across the river, fresh today," he said as he set a plate before each of us.

Wendy shot me an agonized look as I gingerly spooned the first slice into my mouth. She realized that to refuse a taste would be an affront to our host who stood close by, watching our reactions, so she took a bite. Her eyes closed momentarily as the peach slid between her lips, then opened wide in amazement. "Ambrosia," she exclaimed and quickly readied another spoonful.

I followed her lead and raised a dripping slice to my lips, inhaling the unmistakable aroma of sun-ripened peach. The juice was slightly sweetened by a sauce that intensified the natural flavor and left it lingering in the mouth long after the bite was swallowed. "What is the sauce?" I asked.

"*Miel*," he answered.

"That's it? Just honey?"

"Yes. Do you like it?"

I rolled my eyes upward in pleasure as I tried to find the words that could express how marvelous the entire dinner had been. "Perfect," I lamely repeated.

But, the evening was not yet over. Our host came forth, bearing a tray with three snifter glasses of an amber-colored liquid. He placed one in front of each of us and took one for himself. "No charge," he said. "It has been my pleasure to have you in my restaurant tonight."

We raised our glasses in salute and inhaled the heady aroma of Armagnac brandy. There was no mistaking the assertive earthy quality that distinguishes it from its better known cousin, Cognac. It was smooth as syrup as it spread its relaxing warmth throughout the system. Could anyone sip such nectar and still find fault with the world?

Apparently resigned to the evening's unprofitable fate and abandoning his post for good, our host took a chair from the table behind him and graciously asked, "May I join you?"

"Please do," Wendy said.

While he swung the chair around, I decided to take advantage of the moment and our host's willingness to chat and broached a topic that I'd been wondering about during our travels in France. "Can you help me understand why the French are so undecided on the European Economic Community treaty? It seems strange to us that a few French farmers can have such an enormous influence."

"Ah," he began, "that is an easy question." He took a sip of his Armagnac and continued. "You say, 'a few French farmers,' and it is true that officially only about five percent of us are farmers, but what you must know is that all Frenchmen are farmers," he paused dramatically before adding, "here," as he thumped his chest. "It is the dream of every Frenchman to own a farm when he retires from work. Even the politicians have such a dream, and so they vote as if they were farmers." He sipped his Armagnac to give us time to digest his words.

"We have a similar situation in the United States," I said. "Perhaps it began with the same dream of every man tilling his own soil, but it has changed. Now the people crowded into the cities don't even know where milk comes from."

"Too many people make too many problems," he said. "But at least we still eat well in France."

"For that, we are most grateful," Wendy said, raising her glass in a benediction for the evening.

~ On Your Own ~

Montpellier

Montpellier originally boasted the Latin name of "Monspistillarius" (Montagne des Espiciers) when it was first occupied in the 10th century by spice traders. When Languedoc joined France in the 13th century, Montpellier lost its strategic trading position to the port of Marseille, but soon became famous for its University of Medicine.

Attractions

Not only is the view from the **Promenade du Peyrou** marvelous, once there you will be able to explore both the Roman water temple (**Le Château d'Eau**) and **aqueduct**.

Nearby the Esplanade and the place de la Comédie is the **Musée Fabre**, which houses a fine collection of painting and sculpture—

enough to keep you occupied for several hours, if you are willing to spare the time.

Hotels

The **Grand Hôtel du Midi** (22, blvd. Victor-Hugo) is on the place de la Comédie near the Opéra and the old city. Old and comfortable, it provides an ideal refuge from the bustle around it. Some rooms offer air conditioning. Parking is two blocks away near the train station. No restaurant. Rates: 300-480F ($60-96). Phone: 67-92-69-61.

The **Hôtel de Noailles** (2, rue Écoles-Centrales) is in a quieter section, behind the Musée Fabre. The building is from the 17th century, but the rooms and facilities are modern. There is no air conditioning and no restaurant, although in-room breakfast is available. Rates: 280-480F ($56-96). Phone: 67-60-49-80.

Restaurants

Le Chandelier (3, rue Leenhardt) receives a star from Michelin and reservations are a must. Located near the train station on a rather seedy street, the exterior belies the elegance within. Try the chicken salad with peaches for an unusual treat. Menus: 240-360F ($48-72). Closed Sundays, the first three weeks of August, and the first week of January. Phone: 67-92-61-62.

Le Louvre (2, rue Vieille) offers a lighter menu beginning at 120F ($24). Closed Sundays and Mondays and October 15-30. Phone: 67-60-59-37.

Béziers

Béziers has long ties to history, although little remains to remind the tourist of its tempestuous past. A bit of the oldest Roman road in France (the Via Domitia) can be seen at the archaeological digs of Oppidum l'Enserune six miles south of Béziers on route N113. Hannibal's legions left little to mark this as an important Roman outpost in the conquest of Gaul, however; perhaps the Roman roads were not designed to carry elephants. The medieval town was largely destroyed during the Albigensian Crusade, so what now looks old dates from the 13th and 14th centuries.

Attractions

The **Cathédrale de St-Nazaire** looks more like a castle than a church, and for good reason. The original church was burned in 1209 when crusaders slaughtered thousands at the Église de la Madeleine in their search for a few Cathars.

Béziers fills up with bull-fighting aficionados each year around August 15-18 to celebrate (with a bull fight) **La Fête de la Vierge** (the Festival of the Virgin).

The **Musée du Vieux Biterrois et du Vin** has a fascinating display of the construction of the Canal du Midi (1665-81) which connected the Mediterranean to the Atlantic by way of the Garonne River at Toulouse.

In the surrounding area:

If you are not rushed, a short backtrack to the historic city of **Aigues-Mortes** is well worth your time. Take route D62 until the **Tour de Constance,** the central tower of the medieval battlements, comes into view. Admission is 25F ($5).

Follow route D62 back to the *péage* A9/E15 just south of Montpellier where you turn off onto route N112 heading for **Sète.** This is the largest and one of the oldest fishing ports in France, full of activity and good food. During the summer months, nautical jousting entertains the tourists.

A narrow causeway stretches from Sète to the largest playground for sun worshippers in France at **Le Cap d'Agde.** You will feel that you are in a boat rather than a car as you skirt the Bassin de Thau on the one side and on the other, the Mediterranean. As you approach Le Cap d'Agde, you will note the hundreds of campsites and resorts that attract over a million visitors a year to the area. You will have to leave the car and everything else to see the **Quartier Naturiste,** an entire district reserved for nudists, complete with shops, cafés, and expensive apartments.

Hotels

Grand Hôtel du Nord (15, place Jean-Jaurès) is in a surprisingly quiet area despite being located just off the place Jean-Jaurès. No restaurant. Rates: 250-450F ($50-90). Phone: 67-28-34-09.

Hôtel des Poètes (80, allées Paul-Riquet) is right alongside the gardens of le Plateau des Poètes. Quiet and lovely, but small and also without a restaurant. Rates: 175-280F ($35-56). Phone: 67-76-38-66.

Restaurants

Brasserie Ragueneau (36, allées Paul-Riquet) offers standard fare with some interesting Provençal touches. Menus: 125-170F ($25-34). Phone: 67-28-35-17.

La Cigale (60, allées Paul-Riquet) offers substantial food at reasonable rates. The salads are truly enormous. Menus: 110-240F ($22-48). Phone: 67-28-21-56.

Castres

Attractions

If you are an art buff, don't miss Castres' **Musée Goya,** a comprehensive collection spanning 50 years of the artist's paintings.

The **Jardin de l'Evêché** is a sculpted garden designed by André le Nôtre, who is held in high regard for his designs of the gardens at Versailles.

In the surrounding area:

A beautiful side trip, through a region reminiscent of the lower Sierras in California, lies to the east of Castres. Drive into the western area of the **Parc du Haut Languedoc,** following the course of the Agout River through woodsy country with enormous granite boulders scattered haphazardly about. The route provides plenty of secluded picnic areas, so take a lunch. Leaving Castres on route D89, pass through the settlement of Roquecourbe and on to Vabre, where you make a sharp right turn to reach Brassac. At Brassac, again turn right to pick up route D622, which returns you to Castres. The entire circuit covers about 28 miles, so you have plenty of time to stop and tramp around a bit on any of the well-marked trails.

Hotels

The Grand Hôtel (11, rue Libération) is an aging beauty alongside the river, with a lovely view from the restaurant terrace. Unfortunately, the restaurant is closed from June 15 through September 15 as well as Saturdays. The hotel itself is closed from December 15 through January 15. Rates: 210-280F ($42-56). Phone: 63-59-00-30.

The Hôtel Occitan (201, ave. Charles de Gaulle) is located in the new part of town where route N112 becomes avenue Charles de Gaulle.

There's free parking, but no restaurant. Rates: 250-400F ($50-80). Phone: 63-35-34-20.

Restaurants

La Rive Gauche (7, rue Empare) is our much-beloved, two-fork discovery, providing classic French cuisine with a few added touches from the Languedoc. Closed Sundays. Menus: 75-200F ($25-40). Phone: 63-35-68-49.

La Mandragore (1, rue Malpas) is actually located in an ancient château. The stone walls and overhead beams lend a mellow glow to the dining area. The cuisine is classic Languedocien—seafood and lamb, spiced with coriander, oregano, and garlic. Closed Sundays and the first two weeks in August. Menus: 80-240F ($16-48). Phone: 63-59-51-27.

Chapter 8

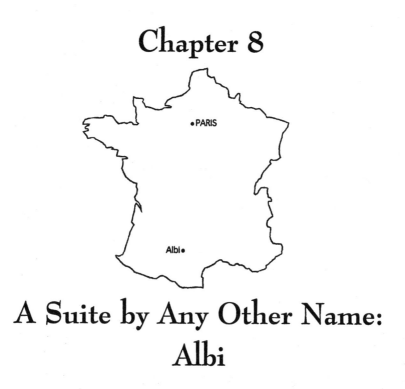

A Suite by Any Other Name: Albi

Wendy stood at the hotel window in Castres, clutching the curtain in one hand as she stared through the glass to where the Agout River flowed. "When we reach Albi, our trip will be almost over," she sighed.

I looked up from where I was putting my shaving gear into the carry-on bag. My razor is always the last thing I pack in the morning because, next to a passport, I consider it the one indispensable item for the male traveler. "Come on," I tried to cheer her. "We still have three glorious nights to spend on the road before we reach Paris."

"I really hate to see it end. Couldn't we keep the car for a few more days?"

"We've already broken all of the rules for the trip," I replied, "but the one rule we can't break is the one laid down by the airline—no changes, no refunds."

"I know," she said and moved away from the window to begin packing her things. "I just hate to let go. It's been such fun."

"Maybe we can find one of those chain motels in Albi. Remember Olivet? That might make you wish the trip was over."

"You wouldn't dare," she threatened, but the smile on her lips contradicted her words. Moments later, Wendy snapped the lock on her bag and declared she was ready to eat breakfast and get back on the road.

The road from Castres to Albi crosses open meadowland interspersed with steep, mountainous ridges which make for a rather tortuous route. One moment we were gliding through lush pastures, but seconds later a sudden turn thrust us into a dark wilderness of steep rocky walls covered with a bramble of brush and scrub oak. The warm dampness of the morning air seemed to hang stagnant within the car, even with the windows open. It took little imagination to conjure visions of brutish *sangliers*, the sabre-tusked wild boar, lying in wait for the hapless traveler who might step into one of those dark tangles of vegetation.

We swung out of the final ravine onto a broad flood plain, dominated by vast fields of sunflowers, the city of Albi a distant rosy glow within the sweeping curve of the river, its cathedral towering above the surrounding town.

As we approached, Albi's Cathédrale de Ste.-Cécile began to appear more like a maximum security prison than a place of worship. Along its sides, round columns of red brick rose to the roof line. The bell-tower continued skyward, resembling a pair of enormous brick chimneys linked together by a solid brick wall. Viewed from a middle distance, no ornamentation was visible to relieve the severity of the lines of the fortress-cathedral, unique in all of France for the history that evoked its conception. We had arrived at the heart of the land against which Pope Innocent III, in 1209, launched the Albigensian Crusade. One gains a sense of history everywhere in Europe, in its ruins and monuments glorifying past civilizations, but you must bring a sense of wondering curiosity to see beyond the stones and statues, to find the roots of darker events that changed the course of humanity.

Three centuries before Luther, the Cathars of southern France had quietly rebelled against Papal authority by denouncing all accumulation of wealth by the church, along with renouncing all pleasures of the flesh for themselves. The Pope, realizing that any sect with such tenets would soon die out from attrition, took little note of the heresy until the counts of Toulouse and Languedoc, in the name of reform, began to oust the wealthy bishops and abbots and divert the church's property to their own secular needs. That was a heresy which could not be ignored.

With the blessing of Pope Innocent III, King Philip II of France encouraged many of the French nobles to join with those from Italy and Germany in the Albigensian Crusade, and stirred by the promise land grants, they proceeded to ravage the Lanquedoc. Béziers was taken, and when the Papal Legate was asked if Catholics should be spared, he answered, "Kill them all, for God knows His own."

Over fifteen thousand men, women, and children were indiscriminately slaughtered, and the town was burned to the ground before the troops moved on against the fortress of Carcassone. A generation later, no one in the area dared to speak against the Church, and the vast domains of Languedoc and Toulouse were added to the realm of Louis IX of France.

There is no monument, no statue in Albi to mark the birth of the Reformation and that of its dark twin, the Holy Inquisition; yet it was here that the two were first conceived. The simple idea that man was answerable to his conscience and the precepts of

Jesus spread throughout all of Europe, challenging the authority, the power, and the privilege of the Church, and leading to atrocities unequalled until our time.

Making our way into the city, we parked the car at the place Vigan, a broad, flat slab of asphalt that seemed to attract the morning's heat and transmit it directly to the vehicles. "Let's find a cool café and have something with ice in it before we start hunting a hotel," Wendy suggested.

A nice, cold beer and a shady table on which to study the guidebook would make the initial phase of the search for a hotel a real pleasure. The second phase, the actual walking in the heat, was best left unthought of as long as it could be postponed. Together, we crossed the narrow street and found a sidewalk café with an open table beneath a tasteful umbrella beer ad.

Ordering a beer and a grapefruit juice took but a moment, and I quickly opened our obsolete red book to the section on Albi. After our embarrassing experience in Castres, I was a bit skeptical when I found several hotels listed that were located within a few blocks from where we sat. "Why don't you wait here while I check out a couple of these?" I asked.

Wendy looked from her frosted glass across the hot, black pavement and graciously consented to my solo excursion. "Don't be long," she said. "It's getting hot."

She was right. By the time I had retraced my steps to the car, perspiration was streaming down my face and my polo shirt clung to my back like a wet rag. The interior of the car was already furnace hot under the unrelenting August sun when I opened the door to toss in my jacket, making me very glad that we were no longer on the road. I walked as briskly as I could across the pavement to the promising shelter of the narrow rue St.-Antoine where the *Michelin* had indicated two hotels were located.

Two doors down from the corner, the first hotel proclaimed its presence with an ancient, weather-beaten sign that displayed a single star. A glance into the dilapidated lobby through the grimy window led me to mutter aloud, "Scratch that one." Across the narrow street, a passing woman gave me a distrustful glance as she hurried to put more distance between us. At another time, I might have been amused, but the heat had become even more oppressive within the lane's cramped confines where every building served to block the movement of air and radiate the stored heat from other days. "Are we having fun yet?" I asked myself, not caring who might overhear.

The thought of Wendy, with a cold drink in hand, sitting under the umbrella with a cooling breeze lightly caressing her skin was tempting me to abandon my search when I saw the heraldic sign of the Hostellerie Saint-Antoine. It beckoned like an oasis in a desert.

The term *hostellerie* is generic, generally placing an establishment rather low on the hotel hierarchy, somewhere between a youth hostel and an *auberge*; so I was delighted to find that this one had been totally refurbished into a four-star, modern hotel. The heavy glass doors opened onto a lobby with gleaming tile floors covered with oriental carpets. Period tables were decorated with elegant floral displays, and only the beamed ceiling gave a hint as to the room's humble ancestry. Best of all, it was cool. The sign at the desk proclaimed that the hotel had been founded in 1734, but now all fifty-six rooms were individually air-conditioned. Sight unseen, I signed for a room.

A handy little map from the desk provided directions to negotiate the back streets to the parking lot and, more important, a short way back to where I had left Wendy. She smiled as I approached and gestured like some grand duchess to the empty chair beside her. "You look hot," she said. "Sit down and have some refreshment."

For a moment, I considered playing the role of casual habitué, but I was too excited about having discovered the hotel. "*Merci*," I said, "but one beer in the morning is enough for me."

I held out my arm. "If her ladyship would be so kind as to accompany me," I mocked, "the car awaits."

"You didn't find anything?" Her breezy affect disappeared in alarm.

"Oh, yes," I answered, "but we'll have to move the car into the *hostellerie* parking lot."

"*Hostellerie?*" She looked shocked. "You didn't really book us into a *hostellerie?*"

"It's not that bad," I said, trying to restrain a grin. "Wait until you see it."

"I hope it has a big window that opens. I can't take much more of this heat," she said as she gingerly settled against the seat that had been roasting in the sun. A few moments later we were in the parking area at the rear of the *hostellerie*. It was sheltered by tall trees, and lush clumps of pink hydrangea were planted against the fence. Wendy was out of the car immediately and stood in the shade as I removed the carry-ons from the trunk.

"We could camp out here, if things get too bad," she said in a tone that may or may not have been joking.

"Come along," I replied, swinging a bag from each hand as I turned the corner from the parking lot to the rear entrance of the hotel. My steps slowed involuntarily, and Wendy stepped on my heel, as we both gazed in amazement at the sweep of lawn, shaded by magnolia, chestnut, and persimmon trees, that greeted us. It was like a tiny park, this *hostellerie* garden, with flowering azaleas and hydrangeas growing in little nooks of deep shade where lounge chairs had been placed to seduce the weary traveler.

"Some *hostellerie*," Wendy said slowly, a dawning appreciation crossing her face. "Is it expensive?"

"I didn't ask. But it's ours for the day and night." I shifted the bags to one hand and dug the room key out of my pocket. "Let's go in."

Our room was larger than a suite at our Paris hotel, complete with a sitting area and color TV, a king-sized bed, private bath and shower, and a large air-conditioning unit that extended beneath the windows. Wendy looked out of the windows onto the garden below while I adjusted the cooling.

"It's heaven," she said and slowly drew the drapes, leaving the room in cool darkness. "We can see Albi later," she said, throwing herself on the bed. "For now, I need a nap."

A crackling boom of thunder awakened us a few hours later. Wendy rushed to the window and pulled aside the drape to look out on the garden. I rose and stood beside her at the window, watching the rain beat upon the trees below. The sky above us was thick and dark, but in the distance, a patch of thin blue dropped a rainbow of curving color toward the ground, indicating that the storm would pass as quickly as it had arrived.

"It should be cooler after this," Wendy said. "Maybe we should do the tourist bit now."

"And eat lunch?"

"First things first," she replied, knowing that with me eating was always first.

It was cooler, and the air smelled fresh and clean as we walked through the renovated ancient part of town toward the cathedral. A small *crêperie*, with outside tables sheltered from the sun by enormous, white umbrellas, beckoned us, and we settled down to a light lunch of mushroom-and-cheese–filled crêpes and glasses of a nameless white wine. Across the square, the enormous bulk of the cathedral seemed to glare down upon us through the malevolent, slitted eyes of its embrasures. The coolness following the storm was quickly giving way to heat with the return of the sun, and although we were reluctant to leave the shelter of the umbrella, we decided to explore the church and museum before the heat became unbearable again.

As we walked slowly along the length of the cathedral, looking up its steep, brick face, broken only by the evenly spaced embrasures, we flinched slightly at the thought of a flight of arrows or a cascade of boiling oil descending upon us from those ugly slits. This was definitely not a beautiful building, but it was truly awesome in its immensity. We turned the corner to the south side and were presented with the elaborate surprise of the portico—a 16th-century addition of wedding cake turned to stone. Spire upon spire reached toward the sky, supported and intertwined with the most delicate tracery of lace carved from stone, the whole so out of keeping with the severity of the rest of the building as to leave the spectator gawking in shock.

Further surprise awaited us within the cathedral where a painting of a modest Adam was joined with that of a saucy Eve who flaunted her charms with abandon, both set within the flamboyant, carved-stone screen around the choir. Smaller paintings of saints and other notables, along with numerous small statues, further adorned this screen. The altar itself boasted a fresco depicting the Last Judgement, with a doleful lot allocated to heaven and seemingly more cheerful group consorting with demons. Renaissance Italy had left its unmistakable mark in the land of the Cathars. Still, the total effect was somewhat like watching fireworks, a dazzling display that catches the eye, but offers little of lasting interest. "Let's go see the Lautrec exhibit," Wendy suggested, finding me all too ready to leave the dissonance of that vaulted hall.

Next to the cathedral stands the 13th-century Palais de la Berbe. An imposing, brick, fortress-like building that would be impressive in its own right if it were not dwarfed by the nearby cathedral, it has been turned into an art museum that features the world's most important collection of the paintings, posters, and drawings of native son Henri Toulouse-Lautrec. Unlike his contemporaries such as Renoir, Sisley, and Monet, Toulouse-Lautrec had little interest in the nuances of light, preferring to delineate his subjects through a few carefully chosen lines. With an eye as accurate as Goya and a hand as sure as Durer, he depicted the seamier side of Parisian life during the Belle Epoque.

The architecture of the *palais*, originally the home of the bishops of Albi, was not ideally suited to function as an art museum, and unfortunately little had been done in the way of lighting to improve the visibility of the displays. We moved from room to room, each filled with an abundant mixture of paintings, drawings, and posters exemplifying the flowering of the arts under the Counts of Toulouse. We quickly tired from overexposure to the magnitude of the exhibit, and as the heat was again becoming oppressive, we decided with a single mind that life back at the *hostellerie* would be far more pleasant.

Back in the luxury of the hotel, memories of the afternoon heat weighed heavily in our choice of a restaurant: the one in the hotel would be just fine. We showered and, for the first time since leaving Paris, it seemed right that I wear a necktie and jacket to dinner.

"Flaunting the luxury of the air-conditioned elite?" Wendy taunted.

"If you got it, show it." I replied, noting that she had donned the flowing black dress I had last seen on the Bateau Mouche in Paris.

The dining room occupied the length of the hotel wing that overlooked the garden. We were seated at a window where we could look out at the banks of azaleas and the massed pom-poms of hydrangeas, selectively lighted by soft floodlights which left parts of the garden veiled in mystery. The restaurant was clean and bright, with starched white linen on the tables and a single large bouquet of mixed lilies and chrysanthemums displayed on a table in the center of the room. Several of the tables were already occupied, and I noted with a certain satisfaction, all of the men were wearing ties, although one had removed his jacket.

We ordered the 130-franc, fixed-price menu, which included hors d'oeuvres of a delicate puff-pastry stuffed with scallops, followed by a clear, country-vegetable soup. The entrée was a specialty of the region, braised saddle of *sanglier* with classic hunter's sauce. A bottle of Bordeaux seemed in order, so we selected a moderately priced St. Emilion which proved to be just right with the rich, tender meat and also went well with the assorted cheeses that followed the salad course. We completed the meal with small raspberry tartlets and coffee. Even with the added expense of the wine, the complete dinner for two was only 400 francs, roughly eighty U.S. dollars.

The following morning, while Wendy was still enjoying the unexpected luxury of the room, I carried our bags down and settled the check. A total of 1370 francs was due, almost three hundred dollars! I looked at the itemized account: 400 for dinner, okay; 120 for breakfast, okay; 850 for the room . . . that was almost one hundred and ninety dollars for a night's lodging! I handed over my credit card, and the charge was duly recorded. "Do you have less expensive rooms?" I asked.

"Oh yes, sir," the clerk answered. For a double our rooms run from 650 to 950 francs per night depending upon the degree of comfort. You had one of the deluxe rooms, of course."

"Of course." I echoed, even as I inwardly cursed myself for not having asked about rates the previous day. The extra fifty dollars was probably for the sitting area and TV that hadn't been used. Chalk another up to experience.

A minute later, Wendy came down, looking happy and rested. "All set?" she asked.

"Ready to go." I answered.

"Was it expensive?"

"Not bad," I replied, and we walked through the garden to our awaiting car.

~ On Your Own ~

Albi

Physical attractions other than the dominating cathedral and the Toulouse-Lautrec museum are few in Albi, but during the spring-summer months the city sponsors three high-quality festivals. The jazz festival in April features musicians of international fame. The theatre festival is held from the last week of June through the first week of July and, if you speak fluent French, is a great time to join the avant garde. Classical music gets its days from the last week in July through the first week of August. The city is more than usually crowded during those periods and accommodations are scant.

Hotels

The **Hostellerie St-Antoine** (17, rue St-Antoine), although centuries old, is thoroughly modernized, and you pay the price for the comfort. Close to everything and with a good restaurant. Rates: 380-950F ($76-190), with free parking. Menus: 150-260F ($30-52). Phone: 63-54-04-04.

The nearby **Chiffre** (50, rue Sere-de-Rivières) also offers some air-conditioned rooms and parking, but lacks a restaurant and a sense of history. Phone: 63-54-04-60.

If you are on a budget, **Le Vigan** (16, place Vigan) is a bargain, but it's without air conditioning. The restaurant offers good value for the price, as well. Rates: 220-330F ($44-66). Menus: 80-200F ($16-40). Demi-pensions: 220-230F ($44-46), just don't expect the 200-franc diner to be included. Phone: 63-54-01-23.

If you plan on visiting Albi during festival time, and don't mind a bit of extra driving, the *auberge* **Noël** (rue Hôtel de Ville) in the small village of Réalmont (halfway between Castres and Albi on route N112) provides a demi-pension that cannot be matched in either of the neighboring cities. Only eight rooms are available, but the restaurant is open to all. Rates: 210-300F ($42-60), dinner included(!), 195-265F ($39-53) without dinner. Menus: 120-250F ($24-50). Phone: 63-55-52-80.

Restaurants

Le Jardin des Quatre Saisons (19, blvd. de Strasbourg) is just across the river from the old city in the direction of Cordes. There is a walkway on the bridge, and the view is worth the walk. Strictly fresh food according to the season is the honestly followed rule here. Closed Mondays. Menus: 120-150F ($24-30). Phone: 63-60-77-76.

Le Moulin de la Mothe (rue de la Mothe) is a fancier place, in an old mill by the River Tarn, but the prices are surprisingly reasonable. Menus: 130-250F ($26-50). Closed for vacations during November and February. Phone: 63-60-38-15.

Chapter 9

Time Travel: Cordes, Villefranche-de-Rouergue, Rocamadour, Souillac, & Brive-la-Gaillarde

We followed the River Tarn on its westward course to the ancient town of Gaillac, passing the ruins of Castelnau-de-Levis that had dominated the area west of Albi until Simon de Montfort brought his army against the Albigensian heretics. Now, the ruined castle lent a romantic aura to the valley, giving no hint of the massacre that followed its fall.

The direct road from Albi to Cordes would have taken only half the time, but it led away from the river and into the barren land at the southern edge of the Causses. On the river road, all was lush and green, with fields of corn and tobacco on the flatland and strips of vineyards layered in contoured rows on the higher ground. The road followed the crest of the hills, and the early morning was still cool. An occasional crow or magpie fluttered in the oaks, protesting the disturbance of its tranquility as we passed. Other than the castle, which remained within sight for several miles, there was no sign that we were visitors to what once had been a dark and bloody land. Gaillac has little to offer the tourist beyond wine-tasting, and it was too early in the morning for that, so we turned northward to Cordes.

Cordes was one of the first of over 300 *bastides* to be built by the French and English during the power struggles of the 13th and 14th centuries. *Bastides* were planned communities, in some respects like the well-advertised, country-estate developments that are sprouting up in the United States today. Heavily fortified to protect the inhabitants from roving brigands, they offered amenities and inducements beyond those of the cities. While present-day developers offer golf courses, the *bastides* featured a central square with a church and sheltered arcades to promote the cultural and commercial life of their citizens. As an added incentive, the towns were given self-rule and, in the case of Cordes, the right to charge a toll for passing through the area. All this so one king or the other could lay claim to the land.

Cordes is unusual; it was established by the Count of Toulouse in 1222 as a Cathar stronghold, supporting neither the French nor English crowns until 1229 when the entire Bas Languedoc, including Toulouse, was awarded to the French in settlement of the Albigensian Crusade. Out of the ordinary in design as well, Cordes took the form of an ellipse, rather than the usual square or rectangle, its walls roughly following the contours of its hilly perch.

We left the car outside the city walls and entered through a high, arched gateway that once had supported heavy doors and an iron grate that dropped from above. The street was cobbled and led uphill through the arcades which were occupied by various shops displaying baskets, leather goods, pottery, and other handcrafts. Bright banners emblazoned with assorted heraldic devices fluttered overhead.

We turned away from the arcades and followed the path along the wall to enjoy the sweeping view. Cordes had expanded very little since its founding, and the farmers still planted right up to the city walls. The faint, sweet aroma of ripening fruit rose from an orchard of peaches that lay just below us, where a solitary man walked between the rows of trees surveying his crop.

We reached the far end of the wall and turned back into the town, walking carefully on the rough cobblestone street. Just beyond the squat, Romanesque church in the center of town, we found a stone building of such harmonious grace as to seem out of place among its companions. The facade consisted of three tiers of arches, each filled with glass set in delicate stone tracery, resembling the architecture of the Pont du Gard, if it were to be adapted for habitation. A sign indicated that this was the location of the tourist office.

Inside, we were told that this lovely building was the original home of the head falconer to the Count of Toulouse, restored in the 19th century to its original form. Only the staircase, which had been added in the 15th century, would have seemed new to the builder. For two francs, one could climb the stairs to reach a museum containing some early drawings, lithographs, and paintings of Cordes. We declined, choosing instead to use our time on further study of the exterior.

"Look up there," Wendy said, "falcons."

I looked skyward, trying to make out the shape of a bird against the bright blue. "Where?" I saw nothing. "Where?"

"The roof!"

There, carved into the stone of each of the abutments supporting the overhang of the roof, was the likeness of a falcon.

Like soldiers standing guard over the house of their general, they had stood at attention through the centuries. We walked down the main street to the car, thinking as we passed under the banners that it is sometimes better to let the past speak for itself, rather than trying to resurrect it with flamboyant flags.

Upon leaving Cordes, we headed northward, through the rustic settlement of Laguepie scattered along the juncture of the Aveyron and Viaur Rivers and on to Villefranche-de-Rouergue. We were well into the Causses now, and ragged edges of the folded mountain ranges gave an unfinished look to the landscape on either side of the Aveyron Valley. Scattered wilderness areas were interspersed with small orchards, and the farmhouses were widely separated from each other until we reached Villefranche.

Originally, the town of Villefranche-de-Rouergue protected the northern edge of the territory controlled by the Count of Toulouse, but it was given over to the French king in 1229. In 1252, Alphonse de Poitiers, brother to the king, abandoned the old site and built a new town across the river from the old. Although the ramparts and fortifications were destroyed following the end of the Hundred Years War, Villefranche-de-Rouergue is one of the best preserved of the classic *bastides*.

We crossed the Aveyron and turned into the well-marked parking area beside the tourist office. Across the street, a beautiful little park invited us to get out of the car and explore the town beyond. I dashed into the tourist office, where I was given a map detailing interesting sites and, most importantly, how to find our way back to the car.

Following the map, we meandered through the promenade du Guiraudet and headed toward the main square. In true *bastide* fashion, the streets were straight and intersected at right angles, so that at each crossing, we could see the full stretch of ancient buildings lining each road. We reached the arcades after only a couple of blocks, although the rough cobblestones made it seem much farther.

Unlike Cordes, the square of Villefranche-de-Rouergue had not been "restored" into an artists' colony. There were no heraldic banners and no sign of fresh concrete and paint. The exposed, oaken beams of the sheltering arcades looked as ancient as the stone pillars supporting them, and the doors and shutters of the shops below seemed to bear the marks of hand tools unknown for centuries. Obviously, repairs had been made as needed to keep everything in working order, but this was no museum; the square was filled with people going about their everyday lives. Although it was now late in the morning, the bakery was packed, and the produce shop seemed busy. Three businessmen in suits were in a heated argument, whether over business or politics, we could not tell, when a loud clatter came from a print shop next door. One of the men broke off in mid-sentence and dashed away. It seemed that time had stood still only selectively.

We started to move along when I felt the touch of a hand on my shoulder and turned to face a tall blonde fellow with a backpack. He was accompanied by a young woman who smiled and asked, "You are American? We heard you talking."

I nodded my head, not sure what to expect.

"Can you tell us where to find the Chartreuse Saint-Saveur?" she asked.

Why had they picked us out of the crowd? The question went unanswered as I held out the map from the tourist office. The young man took it with a smile for a thank-you, and the two studied it for a moment before she jabbed a finger at the lower edge and uttered a squeal of triumph. They traced the route, speaking to each other in a language I didn't recognize—some Scandinavian tongue, I surmised. He handed the map back and thanked me in English, turning to go.

My curiosity could stand it no longer. "Why did you choose us for directions?"

She turned her head back over her shoulder as they walked away, "American tourists always have maps."

Our next stop was the town of Figeac, at the edge of the Dordogne, but actually in the valley of the River Célé. A pleasant town, with broad avenues lined with plane trees, it was perfect for a light lunch. While we dawdled, I proposed a slight detour to take in one of the more-photographed cities of France, Rocamadour.

"Will we spend the night there?" Wendy asked. "I'd like to stay at the same hotel. Remember? The dining room was in an olive grove lit by Japanese lanterns."

"Fat chance. This time of year, the place will be full of French on vacation, but I'd still like to see it again. It would only take an hour or so if we use the elevator."

"What do you mean 'if'? I'm not climbing those stairs!"

Wendy was referring to the 223 steps that pilgrims use to climb the steep cliff leading to the seven churches of Rocamadour. To do it properly, one is expected to kneel at each step, following the example of such notable figures as Richard the Lionheart, Saint Dominic, Saint Bernard, and several kings of France, although it is not recorded that Louis XIV ever made the trip.

Rocamadour's fame originated in 1166 with the discovery of a perfectly preserved corpse in a cave 400 feet up on the Alzou Canyon. Although probably some unknown hermit who happened to die on a bed of alum, in those days of miracles, it seemed obvious that only a saint could be so incorruptible, so the mummified remains were named Saint Amadour. Tales of miraculous cures soon circulated, and the pilgrimage to the site became one of the must-do trips for anyone professing piety and with sufficient means to pay the way. At its peak of fame, the plains below Rocamadour were crowded with as many as 30,000 people a day.

The Hundred Years War, beginning in 1337, brought turmoil to the region, however, and Rocamadour was not spared. Grown wealthy over the years, it was a natural target for any band of brigands, whether English or French, but they were interested only in plundering the treasury.

Hostilities ended with the ceding of the territory of Aquitane to the French in 1453, and Rocamadour began a steady come-back until 1560, when the Wars of Religion began. The Huguenots, in their determination to destroy all semblance of idolatry, seized Rocamadour and vainly attempted to burn the body of St. Amadour. Failing that, they hacked on it with axes and swords, returning it to the earth in bits and pieces, with the dust bestowed upon the wind. In the 19th century, the Bishop of Cahors had the ancient churches rebuilt and a replica of the mummy placed at the original site, in the hopes of restoring Rocamadour to its former glory and profitability.

Taking the turn-off at Gramat for Rocamadour meant that we would bypass St.-Céré, Bretenoux and Beaulieu-sur-Dordogne, each with its own claim upon the tourist's attention, but the desire to revisit Rocamadour overrode any other consideration. Gramat is a small town, but it's very popular with vacationers because of the nearby animal park which displays some animals not seen in ordinary zoos. Wild oxen, *tarpan* (the wild horse from which our domestic horses were developed), and European bison are allowed free range. The temptation to visit was strong, but the line of cars on the road to the park was deterrent enough to keep us on the road to Rocamadour.

The road north from Gramat began with a steep incline as we climbed a thousand feet onto the massive limestone plateau that ran in a solid sheet from the Céré and Lot Rivers to the

Dordogne. Once out of the valley, we were surrounded by miles of scrub oak, dogwood, and small patches of stunted ash trees, the foliage turned a grayish color from too much sun. It became a major event when the landscape was broken by a shepherd's shack in the distance, or the sighting of an unusual outcropping of rock. Although the distance was actually less than fifty miles, it seemed that an endless stretch of time passed before we turned onto the final road, making our descent into the canyon of the Alzou and catching our first extraordinary view of Rocamadour.

We couldn't help stopping at the scenic overlook, although the parking area was nearly filled, and the stone guard rail was lined with people, their cameras clicking away to record a sight that the eye refused to believe. No modern engineer would have the audacity to choose such a place to build. From the tiny settlement lying between two ancient gates on the flat riverbank, the buildings of Rocamadour rose tier upon tier for five hundred feet, straight up the sheer walls of the escarpment, clinging tenuously to every rocky outcropping until reaching the top and the ramparts of the castle.

The town was obscured as we drove away from the lookout until we reached the high metal span that bridged the canyon. There, the view was even more spectacular, but stopping was not allowed on the bridge, so we followed the road to the parking area next to the old castle, now a home for the caretaker clergy. From the ramparts, we had a striking view of the Alzou winding its way between green fields at the bottom of the gorge, while across the way, half-circling Rocamadour, the sweep of the limestone Causse seemed to form a gigantic amphitheater.

The tickets to the elevator were twelve francs apiece. The price seemed steep, but not nearly so steep as the alternative stairway. We dropped straight down to the place St.-Amadour, with its seven churches. We had no interest in the crypt, so we headed directly up the twenty-five steps to the Chapel of Notre-

Dame. An ancient, fragmented fresco to the right of the entrance showed three skeletons in the process of burying three live men, which gave us pause, considering the tons of rock that towered above. Nevertheless, we entered the darkness of the chapel, moving toward the light of a dozen candles flickering on the altar. In the gloom, we could make out the tiny, wooden statue of the Virgin holding her child. This was the miraculous "Black Madonna."

The carving, dating from the 12th century, was little more than two feet high and portrayed the Virgin in a sitting position. The Child sat upright on her lap, without any support from her arms. His face looked peculiarly adult, with none of the roundness associated with babies. Severe and stern, he stared blankly out through the bars of the protective, black cage that enclosed the statue. In the hushed semi-darkness of the sanctuary, we dared not speak, but Wendy touched my arm and gestured toward the door.

Outside, the air was fresh as it rose from the depths of the canyon below. We breathed deeply, clearing our lungs of candle smoke and our senses of claustrophobia.

I looked back and, for the first time, saw the sword jammed into a crevice high above the chapel entrance. "Look," I said, quoting from the guidebook, "Durandal, the sword of Roland."

"Not likely," Wendy replied. "Remember at the end of the 'Song of Roland' where he uses his last strength to break Durandal to keep it out of the Saracens' hands?" Being no match for Wendy's knowledge of literature and remembering the "Song of Roland" from college only as a bore, I nodded agreement.

We entered what appeared to be a rail car for the second half of our descent down the cliff. It was actually a cable car, fitted with seats that swung to a vertical position as the cable payed out, lowering the car to the town below. The angle seemed to be about sixty degrees, and my sympathy went out to those who had chosen the stairway. The ride was smooth and rapid, depositing us outside one of the old gates.

The only street, which stretched from one gate to the other, was lined with merchants trying to sell every knick-knack imaginable to the crowd. Plaster casts of various saints and crucifixes lined shelves adjacent to racks of T-shirts emblazoned with stencils of Rocamadour, while in another shop, we saw miniature copies of Roland's sword stuck in a plaster rock. It was a carnival of tourists gone mad in search of the perfect souvenir. The constant jostling and noise of the crowd quickly became unbearable, and we returned to the elevator.

"Beauty is in the eye of the beholder," Wendy quoted, adding, "and the best way to behold Rocamadour is from a distance."

The entire excursion had taken less than an hour, so we had plenty of time to drive back across the bridge and follow a road leading down into the canyon on the opposite side from Rocamadour. An enterprising young couple had set up a refreshment stand with picnic tables under the shade of tall trees. We ordered two beers and settled back to enjoy the fabulous view in quietude, before pressing on to Souillac.

The experience of dropping down from the high desolation of the limestone Causses onto the fertile plain at the juncture of the Corrèze and Dordogne Rivers was as dramatic as the entrance of the ancient Israelites into the land of Mammon after seven years of desert wandering. Beginning with a small monastery in the midst of a swamp, the Benedictine monks began draining this land in the 13th century. (The name "Souillac" is derived from "souille," which means a bog where boars wallow. I am not too proud to admit that we amused ourselves for some time by exploring its possible relationship to a similar-sounding word used for hog-calling in the United States.) Despite repeated raids by the English during the Hundred-Years-War, the assiduous monks continued their work, transforming the marsh into the rich farmland of today. Now, only their church remains to remind us of these tenacious Benedictines; all the rest of the abbey was destroyed during the Wars of Religion.

With little else than the abbey church to offer in the way of distractions, we soon left Souillac behind. The fields of corn, tobacco and sunflowers abruptly gave way to what we feared would be a long stretch of scrub oak and ash as we ascended another limestone Causse on the road north. The heat of the afternoon became oppressive, even with all of the windows rolled down, and we regretted not having stopped at Souillac for some refreshment. After about a half hour, we began a descent into the lush Brive Basin. There was no quarrel from Wendy as I headed the car into the old city of Brive-la-Gaillarde.

"La Gaillarde" (the bold) was appended to the town's name in recognition of the bravery displayed by its citizens throughout the Middle Ages when it was often under siege. Strategically located between Bas-Limousin and the Perigord on the fertile plain of the Corrèze River, Brive seemed to attract prosperity, as well as the attention of brigands, throughout its history.

The defensive walls which once surrounded the city have been replaced with a broad boulevard. Curiously, it changes its name five times as it circles the old city, leaving the tourist baffled. Fortunately, the road from Souillac leads straight to the Church of Saint Martin at the heart of the ancient town. There we found a handy café and were soon relaxing under a wide umbrella. It seemed an ideal way to study the church across the square, reportedly the place where Saint Martin gave up his life for the Christian cause.

Martin, a Spanish nobleman, was bent on spreading the Word throughout the pagan south of France. In the year 407, he arrived in Brive upon the feast day of Saturnus. Shocked by the pagan display, Martin ran about the town square, smashing whatever idols came within his reach. Incensed by such impious behavior, the crowd promptly stoned him to death and, ultimately, into sainthood.

"This would be a lovely place to stay," Wendy remarked. "Should we look for a hotel?"

"It's a little early," I replied, looking at my watch. It read 4:50, but the urge to move along had returned with the replenishment of vital fluid. "We can probably do better at Tulle."

She nodded and popped a cube of ice into her mouth, her eyes still on the church across the square. "That has to be the strangest mixture of architecture I've ever seen."

Other than the warm tan of the sandstone, there was little to unify the various elements of the exterior. The columns ended with capitals, decorated with carved figures of men and animals, while the ornamentation under the eaves seemed to have been derived from classical Greece. "Probably gone through a number of renovations," I surmised. "Want to go inside?"

"I'd rather find a hotel and take a shower."

"So, if we're finished here, let's move along to Tulle."

That wasn't the answer she had wanted, but Tulle was now fixed in my mind as the place to spend the night. I hated to admit it, but as we drove across the rest of Brive, I was impressed by the harmonious atmosphere engendered by the use of the same sandstone on buildings both old and new, and I harbored silent regrets at my impatience to leave. It was a lovely town, filled with small strips and squares of flowers, demonstrating a pride in both its past and present.

We circled Brive, starting with the boulevard General Koenig and ending with the boulevard du Sajan; before turning right on the road to Tulle. Within twenty minutes, we had crossed the ridge that separates the Brive Basin from the Corrèze Valley and were winding our way downhill to the city of Tulle and a new evening of adventure.

~ On Your Own ~

Cordes

Attractions

The best of Cordes extends along the **Grande-Rue**. Numerous 13th- and 14th-century, pink sandstone houses, with pointed arches above the doors and windows, effectively erase the notion that poverty dominated all medieval life. These were the homes of the dye makers, silk weavers, and leather merchants. The **Musée Charles-Portal** on Portail-Peint (phone: 63-56-00-40) offers a view of a medieval peasant home along with exhibits of artifacts from bygone ages.

Hotels

Cordes offers the **Grand Écuyer** with its one-star, Michelin-rated restaurant. Each of its twelve rooms is completely equipped with air conditioning and even television. Rates: 590-850F ($118-170). Menus: 180-380F ($36-76). Closed from October 18 through March. Phone: 63-56-01-03.

The **Hostellerie du Parc** is another well-appointed hotel, but you have to accept a lovely terrace and garden in lieu of air conditioning. The restaurant provides hearty fare. Rates: 275-420F ($55-84). Menus: 145-260F ($29-52). Closed all of January. Phone: 63-56-00-12.

Villefranche-de-Rouergue

Attractions

On the south side of the Aveyron river on route D122, before you cross over to the ancient *bastide* of Villefranche, you have an opportunity to visit the 15th-century **Chartreuse St.-Sauveur**. Flamboyant in style, it boasts one of the largest cloisters in France, along with a second, much smaller cloister and chapel. Guided tours are offered in July and August for only 3F. Admission is free the remainder of the year, although without a guide.

Immediately after crossing the bridge to the main town, you'll see the tourist office on your left. There you can get a free map showing the general layout of this unspoiled *bastide*, which should be of interest to the student of medieval warfare and defense. Although the walls and battlements constructed in 1099 have long since disappeared, it is an easy matter to reconstruct them in your mind by following the boulevards that have replaced the walls around the town's perimeter. The streets form the classic right-angle grid that permitted rapid deployment of troops to any point along the walls.

At the center of the *bastide*, the **place Notre-Dame** is surrounded by stalls where the everyday traffic of life is still carried out much the same as it was centuries ago. If you are shopping for souvenirs, this is a good place to look.

The facing **Église Notre-Dame**, dating from the 13th century, is dominated by its unusually high bell tower, the result of a rivalry between Villefranche and the town of Rodez. (Rodez won, with a tower of 87 meters, but it took two hundred years for them to beat out Villefranche's 54-meter tower.)

Hotels

The chain-operated **Francotel** (Centre Escale par route D1—take route D1, in the direction of Rodez, about a half mile out of town) is without a restaurant, but otherwise offers all the comfort you could wish for, including air-conditioned rooms. Rates: 240-285F ($48-57). Phone: 65-81-17-22.

The **Hôtel de la Poste** (45, rue du Général Prestat) provides clean, comfortable rooms with all amenities except air conditioning and TV. The food at the restaurant is simple, but very good. Closed November through March. Rates: 170-270F ($34-54). Menus: 75-140F ($15-28), and a demi-pension (dinner, room and breakfast) is available for two at only 240F ($48). Phone: 65-45-13-91.

Rocamadour

Attractions

Within easy walking distance from the ramparts parking lot, Rocamadour offers the **Rocher des Aigles**, a breeding ground for falcons, hawks, and eagles. The entrance fee is 28F (about $6) for an hour's demonstration of falconry.

For those with less sanguinary interests, a short drive on route D36 will take you to l'Hospitalet, where you may take in one of the best views of Rocamadour. 25F ($5) admission to the adjacent **Forêt des Singes** allows you to watch a hundred or so Barbary apes at play. From l'Hospitalet you can also visit the **Jardin des Papillons**, a butterfly sanctuary, admission: 22F ($4.50). Closed October through February.

The **Grotte des Merveilles** is a small cave, located a few steps north of l'Hospitalet, where natural reflecting pools reveal the beauty of stalactites and stalagmites and paintings that date back some 25,000 years. This is a truly lovely spot and should not be missed by those who enjoy effortless spelunking.

Hotels

The **Beau-Site et Notre-Dame** (rue Roland-le-Preux) is housed in the remains of a 15th-century castle overlooking the Val d'Alzou. The stone walls and heavy beams would seem oppressive were they not countered by cheerily efficient light fixtures, unknown in the original. The excellent restaurant offers dining on the terrace, so you can enjoy the sweeping panorama while you relax. Rates: 340-460F ($68-92), with free parking. Menus: 95-250F ($19-50). Closed from November 12 until the first of April. Phone: 65-33-63-08.

The **Annexe Relais Amadourien** does not have the charm of a medieval castle, but the rooms are large, fresh, clean and air-conditioned. It is an annex of the Hôtel du Château (located about a mile away on the route du Château), but without a view, it commands a lower price. Dinner is served by lantern light in an orchard across from the annex. Rates: 200-265F ($40-53), with free parking. Menus: 68-240F ($14-48). Closed from November 8 through April 8. Phone: 65-33-62-22.

Souillac

Souillac is strategically located as a base camp for anyone wishing to explore the wonders of the Dordogne region.

Attractions

In Souillac, the ancient abbey **Église Ste.-Marie** is particularly notable for the Romanesque sculptures on the west door, flanked by two bas-reliefs of unusual sensitivity. On the right panel, various carnal sins are shown; the central panel reveals a scene from Hell, with grotesque beasts feeding upon each other; and the left panel depicts Abraham's sacrifice of Isaac.

In the surrounding area:

The town of **Sarlat-la-Canéda** lies west of Souillac. Take route D703 for a short scenic drive along the Dordogne river. The **Vieille Ville** has been carefully restored, and the ochre sandstone used in most of the construction provides a warm glow despite its being scrubbed. Many of the twisting lanes around the **Cathédrale St.-Sacerdos** and the nearby **place de la Liberté** are lighted at night by torches, heightening the illusion that Sarlat has escaped the modern world. Note: As would be expected of such a charming town, food and lodging here are the most expensive in the Dordogne region.

Les Eyzies, located amidst the many major cro-magnin sites along the Vézère river, about twenty minutes out of Sarlat on route D47, is home to the **National Museum of Prehistory**. Three floors of paleontology are capped by a gorgeous view of the Vézère river valley. Open all year. Admission: 17F ($3.50). Phone: 53-06-97-03.

Martel, founded in the 8th century to celebrate Charles Martel's victory over the Saracens, is only ten miles from Souillac on route D703. The town is also significant to history buffs as the stronghold of Henry Short Coat, the eldest son of England's King Henry Plantagenet. Only a few touches remain to indicate the heavy fortifications which once surrounded the double-walled town. The Gothic church **St.-Maur** still has two towers crowned with battlements, and the **Hôtel de la Raymondie** retains a turret at each corner from when the fortress was remodeled into a law court in the 14th century. In the center of the town square, a large, wooden, covered **marketplace** is one of the town's more interesting features, although it dates only from the 18th century.

The **Gouffre de Padirac** was famed in ancient times as the entry to Hell, although it was used as a safe hiding place for peasants during the Wars of Religion. Today, two elevators provide easy access to more than a mile of caverns, carved from the limestone by an underground river. You should consider taking along rain gear, because the underground waterfalls create considerable spray. The guided tour (half by boat, half on foot) takes over 90 minutes and costs 23.50F ($5). The site is easily reached from Martel—take route N140 south about ten miles, then turn east on route D673.

If you continue on D703 beyond Martel for another twenty minutes, you will reach **Castelnau-Bretenoux**, with its enormous red castle perched on the heights above the village of Prudhomat. This is one of the largest fortresses in France, with a perimeter of more than three miles, and it's a classic of medieval defensive architecture. When the baron of Castelnau was at the peak of his power in the 12th century, the castle housed 1,500 troops and 100 horses. Admission: 16F ($3). Closed Tuesdays and the months of November and December.

Hotels

The **Grand Hôtel** (1, allée Verninac, Souillac) offers the best combination of good food and lodging, but has no parking facilities. Rates: 210-350F ($42-70). A demi-pension may be had for 230-300F ($46-60). Menus: 100-250F ($20-50). Closed from November 1 to April 1. Phone: 65-32-78-30.

The **Vieille Auberge** (on the place Minoterie, Souillac) does offer free parking, but the hotel rates seem to absorb the savings. Rates: 265-330F ($53-66). Demi-pension is 350F ($70). Menus: 135-250F ($27-50). Closed November 15 through April 1. Phone: 65-32-79-43.

Puy d'Alon (ave. Jean Jaurès, Souillac) is without a restaurant, but has everything else, even parking. Rates: 210-350F ($42-70). Phone: 65-37-89-79.

Brive-la-Gaillarde

Over the centuries, Brive has grown in concentric circles around the old Centre Ville, and the main highways all go directly to the original barricades, now transformed into a broad avenue. As we discovered, the only problem is that the name changes as you circle the town center, so that blvd. Lachaud becomes blvd. Koenig in one direction and blvd. Jules Ferry in the other. Don't despair. Keep your eye on the dome of the Église St-Martin, and you will reach your destination.

Attractions

The **Église St.-Martin** was originally Romanesque, but after centuries of additions and reconstructions, only the apse and transept remain to remind us of the early building. Phone: 55-24-10-82.

You will be astonished at the number of turreted houses that line the streets around **place de Charles de Gaulle**. Some of the most remarkable manors date back to the 13th century, when a man's house was truly his castle.

The **Hôtel de Labenche** (once a 16th-century residence) houses the Musée de Brive and collections of art and artifacts covering the entire history of Brive from the Gallo-Roman to the present. Admission is 24F ($4.80). Closed Mondays and Tuesdays. Phone: 55-24-19-05.

Hotels

The recently refurbished **Truffe Noir** (22, blvd. Anatole-France) has all the aspects of a luxury hotel except the price. Located on the perimeter of the Vieille Ville, it is handy to parking as well as all the sights. In addition, the restaurant is excellent. Rates: 460-600F ($92-120). Menus: 155-270F ($31-54). Phone: 55-92-45-00.

The **Hôtel Quercy** (8, bis quai Tourny) is on the bank of the Correze River, away from the traffic and noise of the main town. Less expensive than the Truffe Noir, it is almost its equal in amenities, lacking only a restaurant. Rates: 310-330F ($62-66). Phone: 55-74-09-26.

For an adventure, you may want to try the **Champanatier** (15, rue Dumyrat), a small hotel in the Vieille Ville that offers a clean room and little else. Rates: 80-250F ($16-50). The hotel restaurant has menus ranging from 80-250F ($16-50) and a demi-pension for 185F ($37). Closed all of February and July 5 through July 20. Phone: 55-74-24-14.

Chapter 10

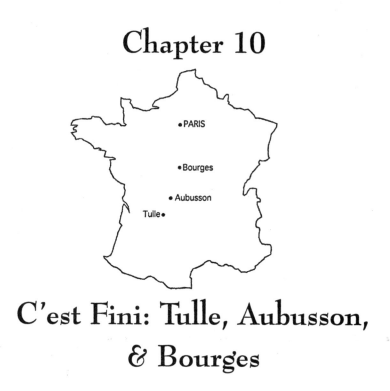

C'est Fini: Tulle, Aubusson, & Bourges

Tulle is not a major tourist town, so even though it was nearly five-thirty when we parked, we were able to find a hotel room overlooking the quiet flow of the Corrèze. While Wendy freshened herself before the mirror, I slid open the doors leading to the balcony and stepped out to savor the view. The Corrèze was indeed quiet; in fact, it was stagnant and covered by a thick green scum, an observation that was pointedly emphasized by a mosquito on my neck. I slapped it hard, and Wendy let out a cry of anguish.

"Oh, no!"

"It's all right. I got him," I said as I examined the smear of blood on my hand. "I guess we'd better close the screen, though."

"No—my *comb*," Wendy replied, holding out a misshapen mass of brown goo for my inspection. The acrid smell of acetone permeated the room. "The top leaked on the nail polish remover. I thought I had it on tight, but it leaked and dissolved my comb."

"Here, use mine." I pulled my comb from my pocket.

Wendy took the comb in her free hand, weighing it against the blob in her other. "I'd never get my hair done with this," she declared firmly, dropping my comb on the dresser behind her. "I need a big one like this." She held up the brown blob for a moment, then amended her statement. "I mean, like this was."

"No need to get upset. We'll buy you another tomorrow."

"Tomorrow? I couldn't go anywhere looking like this."

She had just traveled 200 miles looking like that, but I knew better than to say it. "I'll see what I can do," I said. "Maybe I'll see a restaurant while I'm at it."

"Find a comb first, or we can forget the restaurant," she said as I hurried out.

Fortunately, a sign with the unmistakable green cross emblematic of a pharmacy was visible two blocks away. "Piece of cake," I thought as I adjusted my pace to the slight incline, unaware of an elderly man who was rapidly overtaking me.

"*Bonjour, monsieur*," he said, passing without breaking stride. "*Je fait la promenade toujours à cette heure.*" I was so surprised by his sudden appearance that he was three steps ahead of me before I could translate his words. Why had he even bothered to speak, let alone explain that he always took a walk at that time? Was I intruding on some private preserve, or was he just a lonely old man seeking human contact in a world too often neglectful? My questions would never be answered, because he was far up the hill before I could respond with a "*Bonjour, monsieur*" of my own.

The pharmacy was small, attended by a single clerk who was busy with another customer. I quickly spotted the cosmetic section under a large poster of a nude young lady extolling the virtues of a sun lotion. Next to a row of hair-set gels and sprays was a jobber's rack with nail files, emery boards, nail polish, hair curlers, and hair brushes, each hanging from its appointed hook. I also saw the empty hooks below the brushes, a space that logically should have been filled with combs.

The clerk had now finished with her customer and approached me. "*Bonsoir, monsieur. Vous désirez?*"

"*Bonsoir, mademoiselle. Parlez-vous anglais?*" I couldn't think of the French word for comb, but the linguistic challenge might have been avoided if only she spoke English.

"*Non, monsieur,*" she answered with the finality of a proctor passing out booklets for a final examination.

I fumbled in my pocket for my comb, thinking that I could hold it up and say "*Pour une dame.*" Keys and coins came to hand, but no comb; it was back in the hotel on the dresser where Wendy had dropped it. I pointed at a brush as the next best thing and said, "*Comme ça, mais avec les dents.*" Like that, only with teeth.

She looked puzzled for a moment and then broke out laughing. "*Vous désirez un peigne.*" Her glance shifted to the rack and its empty hook. "*C'est dommage. Il n'y en a plus. Peut-être la semaine prochaine.*"

No more combs? Maybe next week? I couldn't wait until next week, I needed a comb now! Thoroughly rattled, I asked if there was another pharmacy nearby, and she graciously took me to the door and pointed back the way I had come. Four blocks and turn left—couldn't miss it. I then asked her to repeat the French word for comb which I had forgotten as soon as I heard it.

"*Pei-gne,*" she coached me slowly.

"Pay-n-yah," I tried.

She laughed again as she turned back into the shop, and in response to my heartfelt "*Merci, mademoiselle,*" I thought I heard, "*C'est incroyable.*"

As I loped down the hill, I formulated the phrase that I would need at the next pharmacy: *Je voudrais acheter un peigne pour une dame*. I repeated the phrase over and over again, mouthing the words in time with each step, until I was sure that I had it right.

The street into which I had been directed was cobblestoned and very wide, forming the courtyard for the cathedral and the entrance to the ancient section of Tulle. Two narrow streets led into a curving maze of alleys lined with stone buildings, which seemed to lean precariously, while a third street rose above the level of the others by a series of steps. At the top of the steps, I once again saw the reassuring sign of the green cross. I stopped for a moment before entering the shop in order to repeat the magic phrase: *Je voudrais acheter un peigne pour une dame*. I opened the door and stepped in.

A thickset man with heavy brows peered at me through the glass enclosure at the back. "*Oui, monsieur?*" he questioned.

"*Je voudrais acheter une dame pour un peigne*," The phrase poured out with surprising ease, but was hopelessly out of sequence. I had said, "I want to buy a woman for a comb."

"*Qu'est-ce que vous dites?*" With obvious suspicion, and remaining safely behind his glass barricade, he asked me to repeat myself. His Gallic sense of chivalry was obviously outraged by such a request from a foreigner.

"*Un peigne*," I repeated the magic word.

He stepped out of the enclosure, a short ugly club swinging menacingly from his hand. Keeping his eyes on me, he placed the cudgel on top of a stack of drawers with a bang, as though to emphasize its solidity. When I made no move, he seemed to relax a bit.

"*Un peigne?*" I pleaded.

He rubbed his chin as though in deep thought; then he opened one of the drawers and fingered the contents without looking. "*Le voilà.*" In his hand he now held a cellophane-wrapped tortoiseshell comb. I expected him to hand it to me, but he only waved it before my eyes while he spoke in rapid-fire French. The only thing that I could understand was that the comb was, beyond all doubt, top quality.

I held out my hand, but he pulled the comb back. "*Soixanteseizefrancs.*"

I knew they were numbers, knew it was the price, but my mind refused to function as it began counting numbly: *un, deux, trois* . . .

I handed him a fifty-franc note, thinking that he would hand back some change and never be the wiser. Instead, his eyes narrowed and, in the tone of a man who suspects that he is being cheated, he repeated, "*Soixanteseizefrancs,*" then sternly added, "*Encore de l'argent.*"

I fumbled in my wallet and produced a diminutive twenty-franc bill, which I offered to him, feeling like a child buying peace from the school bully. His expression changed from suspicion to irritation as he grabbed a notepad from the counter and, in a sweeping script, wrote "76." The sight of the number was like an electric shock, jump-starting my brain. It quickly sorted out his words into *soixante*, which was sixty, plus *seize*, sixteen, making a total of seventy-six.

I fished up a ten-franc coin, took the comb, the four francs change, and beat a hasty retreat, my mind now caught up in an endless loop of *soixanteseizefrancs*.

Back at the hotel, Wendy was delighted with her new comb. She read aloud from the sticker, "*Véritable tortue.* Genuine tortoise—was it a lot of trouble?"

"Not really," I said, "Gave me a chance to practice my French."

The next morning we set off early, following the road signs northward to Ussel, a town of no particular claim to fame, but on a route that provided a detour around the industrialized bustle of Clermont-Ferrand on the way to Bourges, our final destination for the day. The countryside rapidly became wilder, with dense stands of birch and chestnut bordering the numerous small creeks, leaving the steeper slopes to the pines and junipers. Limestone outcroppings formed ridges that turned into ledges, with fern-lined caves beneath in the dark ravines. It was a harsh and bitter land that offered nothing to a settler, and the few homesteads we saw looked small and bleak.

The next settlement, Egletons, made a brave show, with a few planter boxes of geraniums and a small hotel which proudly bore the name of Ventadour, once the site of the most refined court in all of Europe. At the time when Richard the Lionheart was bashing the Saracens, music and poetry were promoted by the viscounts of Limousin, and the romantic ideas of courtly love and chivalry first took root at Ventadour.

Bernard de Ventadour was the most famous of troubadours. (Not to be confused with minstrels, who only performed the works of others, a troubadour was, like the Calypso singers of today, both composer and performer, able to write a lovely ballad and set it to music at the whim of whichever lady he might be entertaining at the moment.) Although Bernard took his name from the castle in which he was born, early in his career he was forced to find another place to call home. His talents with the women of the court were too much for the viscount to abide. Fortunately, his fame had spread, and he ended his days entertaining the likes of the Duchess of Normandy and the Queen of England.

We made the short detour to take in the exceptional view from the crumbled ramparts of the Château de Ventadour. Looking off into the distance, we seemed eye to eye with eagles, while below, the green of the forest shivered in the strong wind rising from the valley. "Ventadour" (love of wind) seemed a most appropriate name for the castle. Perched above the gorges of the Luzege, the 12th-century fortress appeared impregnable, although it fell to the English during the Hundred Years War and served as their headquarters for thirty years. At the beginning of Louis XIV's reign, the drafty old castle was abandoned by the viscount for more comfortable quarters in nearby Ussel.

Having seen the feudal residence of Ventadour, we made it a point to stop in the beautifully preserved town of Ussel to examine the viscount's 16th-century replacement. Just before entering the old part of the town, we saw a broad square surrounding a stone pedestal that was surmounted by a carved stone eagle. Always curious, we pulled over into the parking area to see what it was commemorating. The lady at the nearby tourist bureau enlightened us somewhat. The eagle was an ancient Roman artifact that had been found several miles away, transported to Ussel, and for lack of any other ideas, mounted in the town square. Sometimes, rather than knowing such things, it is better to let the imagination provide stories of an enchanted eagle's rescue of a fair maiden from dragons. We were advised to leave the car and walk the few blocks into Ussel's old town where the Hôtel de Ventadour dominated its own square.

Visits to the interior of the Hôtel de Ventadour were not permitted, but the exterior, with large ornamental doors and fancy turrets, was as elegant as anything at Versailles. No wonder that the viscount had to apologize to Louis XIV for such splendor and explain why he had abandoned the Château de Ventadour with the words, "All the straw from all the royal palaces would not be enough to fill the chinks in that castle." It did not pay to outdo the king.

Back in the car, we found the sign pointing to Aubusson and turned onto the narrow road that gradually climbed into the hills. Within a few miles, the countryside broadened into flat stretches of grassland, relieved by an occasional series of rolling hills, each capped with a jagged crest of stone. Patches of red poppies added a touch of color to an otherwise green-and-gray vista. We had reached the stark and beautiful Plateau de Millevaches. It seemed that little had changed in this area from the simple existence it had known in the Middle Ages; the few farms we passed had thatched roofs, sitting like weathered haystacks atop the low piles of stone that formed their walls.

Rolling on across the plateau, we were steeped in the sense of isolation, and it was a relief when the road began to descend into the valley of the Creuse River. The charming little town of Aubusson, nestled in a curve of the river, lay just ahead.

I am firmly of the belief that Aubusson was designed with photographers in mind. The town is full of turrets, peaked roofs, and well-kept old houses with skeins of multi-colored wool drying in their windows. The art of tapestry, having brought fame to Aubusson through the ages, is still practiced today in numerous small workshops locally, and tourists are welcomed by many of the artists to observe the weaving process. The most popular tapestry subjects currently seem to be reproductions of famous paintings, particularly the works of Matisse and Picasso, although copies of the famous "Damsel and the Unicorn" are for sale in many shops.

Aubusson has two museums one devoted to this delicate art. One, the Maison du Vieux Tapissier, features examples dating from the fifteenth century; the other is the Hôtel de Ville, where contemporary works are highlighted along with a film explaining the history of tapestry weaving. Since it was too early for lunch and, having already seen the most famous of the Aubusson tapestries, the "Damsel and the Unicorn," in the permanent collection of the Cluny museum in Paris, we decided to press on to Montluçon.

In the 14th century, the castle of Montluçon, home of the Dukes of Bourbon, was strategically built on the crest of a hill overlooking the River Cher. The medieval structure, looking mostly like a squared-off dungeon, may lack the size and grandeur of Renaissance-style Ventadour, but there seems to have been some effort to dress up the main portico with intricate tile work along its facade.

The steep climb to the castle had taken a toll on our energy, and we descended at a more leisurely pace, taking time to admire the meticulous job of restoration the town had done on its 15th- and 16th-century houses. The old town which surrounds the castle has been maintained and renovated to 20th-century standards, and it's probably in better shape today than it has been in any of the last six hundred years. It was all beautiful, but the patina of age had been removed when new roofs, doors, and window shutters replaced the originals. Even the stones looked new, without a trace of lichen or ancient ivy on the walls. The restorers, somehow, had managed to throw the baby out with the bathwater. Although the houses were occupied, there remained a feeling of unreality, like walking through a stage set.

We stopped for a brief lunch at a charming café. Munching on the long, buttered slabs of baguette, lavishly filled with tender ham, we watched other tourists as they joyfully pointed out a unique rain spout or the geometric alignment of some chimneys, anything that would make the perfect snapshot to enhance their memories of this too-picturesque town.

Upon leaving Montluçon we traveled northward, following the course of the Cher. Now the land became more benevolent, the farmhouses looking well maintained and the landscape dominated by stretches of conifer tree farms interspersed with lush pastures. We were delighted with our first sight of an orchard.

Along our route, the small town of Saint-Amand-Montrond reportedly had an ancient abbey and a château that were worth visiting, but neither was in the town, and each would have required a separate detour. Choices had to be made, and we were anxious to get settled in Bourges with enough daylight remaining for some exploration, so Saint-Amand-Montrond was soon left behind us.

Imperceptibly, the landscape became nearly flat, with only an occasional hill to remind us of the wilderness through which we had traveled. Sweeping wheat fields, now only stubble after the harvest, had replaced the bracken, scrub oak, and pine of the Auvergne.

We had reached the southern edge of the fertile lands that stretch north into Burgundy and west into the Loire Valley. This rich farmland over the centuries has financed the dukes of Anjou, Burgundy, and Berry, giving them powers exceeding those of the king. Our route crossed over the *péage* that connects Clermont-Ferrand with Orléans, and the overpass provided our first glimpse of the cathedral towers in Bourges, the onetime capital of Aquitane.

We drove directly into the ancient city, with the towering cathedral as our beacon. The Hôtel de la Poste was located almost in the shadow of the church and, despite its age and only a three-star tourist-office rating, offered us a clean room with a shower and private toilet for 180 francs, about thirty-five dollars. Often such accommodations, equal to or better than what is offered at four-star hotels, are available in even one-star hotels, but you have to ask for them. The desk clerk directed me to a side street, about a half-block away, where overnight parking was permitted. Once that was settled, we were free to roam the city.

Bourges is still the principal city of the Berry Region, but the modern highway system bypasses it, leaving it little visited by tourists. Originally called "Avaric," its strategic position at the confluence of the Auron and Yevre Rivers made Bourges one of the prime objectives of Julius Caesar in his war against the Gauls. After its defeat, the name was Latinized into "Avaricum," and ultimately it became a semi-autonomous city until Roman rule collapsed in the 4th century.

During the Dark Ages, the city's Roman walls were reinforced for protection against marauders, and the name "Bourges" (market town) was adopted to indicate its prominence as the primary trading center for the area. Construction of the local cathedral was begun in 1185, but not completed until the 14th century. In 1360, the Duke of Berry made Bourges his capital, and for the next fifty years, it was the artistic center of France.

The Cathédrale Saint-Étienne was modeled after Paris' Notre Dame, but to the casual eye there is little similarity beyond the imposing grandeur of both. The two towers at Bourges are of unequal height and appear to have been designed by men of divergent views. The right tower is solid and dour, reminding one of the landscape of the Auvergne, while the left tower soars above the other, with lace spires and fanciful decorations, as though representing the bountiful country to the north. The towers present a fine chance to see how the evolution of church architecture moved from Gothic toward Renaissance style. The cathedral's main entrance is raised some twenty feet above the surrounding cobblestone courtyard, and the steps can be a real hazard if your eyes remain fixed upon the towers as mine were. Only Wendy's steady hand saved me from leaving some skin on the stone.

The high arch above the main door depicts the Last Judgement, each detail chiseled with loving care. The demons are anatomical monstrosities, while the humans are anatomically correct: artistic prudery would have to await another place and time. Included among those unfortunates sitting in a boiling caldron is a figure wearing a Bishop's mitre, perhaps a silent, but lasting protest from an underpaid stone carver with a sense for the comic.

The high, vaulted, stone interior is more reminiscent of Amiens than of Notre Dame, and the lovely panels of stained glass, particularly those behind the altar, are a match for those of Sainte-Chapelle in Paris. Perhaps the Cathédrale Saint-Étienne's most distinctive departure from the usual Gothic fare is the absence of a transept and interior dome, leaving the full length of the vaulted chamber unbroken.

We were too late to make the climb up the tower to the bells, and also too late to descend into the crypt containing the tombs of the Dukes of Berry. Still, neither of us felt deprived, and we left the cathedral with the feeling that the obligation to see everything had been miraculously lifted from our shoulders.

It was barely past six o'clock, far too early to think about dinner, but we stopped in front of an attractive restaurant on our way to the palace of Jacques-Coeur. Menus always make interesting reading, and this one had an item that immediately caught my eye. "*Grenouille!*" I exclaimed. "In all the times we have been to France, we've never had frog legs."

"This will be one more time, as far as I'm concerned," Wendy replied, but I had already marked the location of the restaurant in my mind.

The home of Jacques-Coeur is probably the most extravagant private Gothic dwelling in all of France. Building began in 1443 while Jacques-Coeur was finance minister to Charles VII. An arms merchant, with contacts from Damascus to Paris, he instituted a direct levy on all subjects of the King to support a French army, thereby cutting the king's feudal dependency upon the good will of the various dukes and counts. Being an arms merchant, even then, was a lucrative business, and the palace was thought to have cost over 100,000 gold pieces before it was completed in 1457.

The building is roughly rectangular, with one of the long sides built to resemble a medieval fortress, complete with towers and slotted windows. The other side resembles a fancy Italian villa, complete with balconies and much ornamentation featuring hearts (from his name) and scallop shells (*coquilles* St.-Jacques). Midway, a false window is carved into the stone with a bas relief of the master and mistress looking out to where there once had been a statue of Charles VII on horseback. Unfortunately, the statue, like the royalty it represented, was destroyed in the Revolution.

At either end of the building lay the courtyards. One was rather austere, obviously designed as an entrance for servants and tradespeople, while the other was an elaborate facade with a central hexagonal tower, flanked on either side by slate-covered gabled roofs. The tower itself was lavishly embellished with carvings of date and orange trees, presumably to remind one that the owner had voyaged to countries where such exotic plants grew. We would have enjoyed a tour of the interior, but the house had closed for the night at six o'clock and would not be reopened until nine the following morning.

After a quick shower and a change of clothes back at the hotel, we were ready for our last evening in the country before returning to Paris and the flight home. Bourges was the perfect city for a final fling, with its picture-card buildings, balmy weather, and a population that obviously enjoyed an evening promenade.

The street was filled with people, strolling along, casually greeting friends as they passed or cleaning up after their dogs with small shovels and plastic bags. In Bourges, the dog population seemed to outnumber the children by two to one, but each was equally well behaved. With so many people on the street, I was becoming apprehensive about our lack of reservations at my chosen restaurant, and only Wendy's calm assurance restrained me from bolting ahead. "Look," she said, "No one's going any-where. They're just wandering around, talking with friends."

Of course, she was right. Although the front tables with a view of the street were filled, we were quickly seated at a table near the center of the restaurant. While we looked over the menu, we sipped glasses of the *vin de maison*, a lovely, fruity Sauvignon Blanc that was produced locally. The menu was more extensive than I remembered, but we were not hurried to make a selection, and it was pleasant to sip the wine and leisurely savor the names under each course.

Finally, we made our choices. Starting with a plate of cru-dités, we quickly moved to the entrées, and at last I had my *grenouilles* ordered. Wendy settled for roast pork, remaining firm in her conviction that anything with bug eyes and a slippery, green skin was not fit to eat. We left the choice of wine to the waiter, and he produced a bottle of red from Chinon. Made only a few years earlier, it had the fresh fruitiness of Beaujolais Nouveau, but with a softer finish.

The supreme moment arrived when the waiter carried in two covered plates. He served Wendy with a flourish as he removed the cover to reveal several slices of pork resting on a brown gravy and surrounded with small pan-roasted potatoes. She smiled her pleasure as the aroma drifted upward. Next, he placed the second plate before me and, with an identical flourish, removed the cover. Wendy's eyes widened and a look of horror flashed across her face. I looked down at the plate of *grenouilles* and managed a brave smile until the waiter had made his departure.

"You're not going to eat that?" Wendy demanded.

I could only stare at the plate. I had expected five or six large frog legs as are commonly served in the oriental restaurants at home. Instead, I had a plate with perhaps twenty to thirty tiny frogs, skinned and decapitated, but looking for all the world like a pile of miniature human corpses. Their legs were in an extended position and their little arms were crossed upon their bony chests as though arranged by a mortician prior to entombment.

"I can't even look," Wendy said in a sepulchral tone.

"You'd better not," I said as I prepared to do what had to be done. While she pretended to be toasting someone in the front of the restaurant, I carefully separated the legs from each frog and removed the bodies to my bread plate where I gave them burial under several slices of bread. "Now you can look," I said, and she cautiously turned back.

"You're still going to eat those?" She eyed the small pile of legs on my plate.

"Yes," I answered. "Fortunately, there's not a whole lot left to eat."

"Please hurry and get it over with, so that I can enjoy my meal." She must have noticed my hungry look at her pork, because she added, "You can fill up on bread."

Actually, I decided the flavor wasn't bad, as I slipped the meat off into my mouth from each tiny bone, but I resisted Wendy's suggestion about the bread, knowing what would be revealed if I lifted a single slice. It took the cheese course to set things right, and it was the waiter's turn to look aghast as I piled my plate high with hunks from his *plateau de fromages*.

Early the next morning, we set off for Paris, driving through the breadbasket of France, across the Loire to the tourist trap of Fontainebleau without a stop. We had planned a brief rest near the château at Fontainebleau, but the crowds were so thick that we drove on.

"It will feel like being home to get back to Paris, even for one night," Wendy said.

"Do you wish we'd stayed in Paris?"

"Oh, no. In fact, I want to do this again."

"Noel and Marjo want to go with us next time."

193

"I know," she answered. "So do Bruce and Donna, and Bill and Sharon. They all think we're experienced travelers."

"Long on experience, but short on wisdom."

"You're getting too philosophical." She put on her sternest expression. "Now answer me. Can we do it again?"

"On two conditions," I said.

"Too hard to live up to three?" She couldn't resist that jibe. "What are they?"

"One, I choose the itinerary."

"Okay, what's the second?"

"You drive." That was a jibe I couldn't resist.

"If I drive, I get to make the rules, right?"

I felt the trap closing, but could not avoid it. "And what might those be?" I asked.

"First, we drive no more than two hours without a break."

"Sounds reasonable," I said cautiously.

"Second, we travel only on back roads—never on a high-speed *autoroute*. Third, we stop to find a place to stay before 4:00 in the afternoon."

"Haven't we had this conversation before?" I asked.

She gave me that enigmatic smile, and even without an answer, I knew the trap had been sprung. *C'est la vie.*

~ On Your Own ~

Tulle

Although Tulle offers the tourist little of historical significance, it is a pleasant town and a good base from which to explore south to the Dordogne, west to Perigueux, or north to Limoges.

Attractions

The picturesque **Quartier Ancien** includes the 12th-century **Cathédrale Notre-Dame** and the 15th-century **Maison de Loyac**, with its remarkable friezes depicting stags, lions, and even porcupines.

Hotels

The **Toque Blanche** (place Martial Brigouleix) is located outside the main town on route N120 leading to Aurillac. The hotel, with its excellent restaurant, is alongside the river, and the outdoor area is perfect for lunch. There are only ten rooms, so a call ahead is advisable. Rates: 190-225F ($38-45). Phone: 55-26-75-41.

The **Hôtel Royal** (70, avenue Victor Hugo) is located within easy walking distance of the Quartier Ancien, but it's small and lacks a restaurant. Rates: 160-275F ($32-55). Phone: 55-20-04-52.

Restaurants

The restaurant at the hotel **Toque Blanche** (place Martial Brigouleix) is well worth the short drive out of town. Veal and rabbit are featured items. Menus: 145-225F ($23-45). Phone: 55-26-75-41.

The **Central** (32, rue Jean Jaurès) is located in town, on the second floor of a building just across the river from the Hôtel Royal. Both food and service are good. Phone: 55-26-24-46.

Aubusson

Attractions

The **Musée Departmental de la Tapisserie** is located at a wide bend of the River Creuse at the Centre Culturel Jean-Lurcat. The museum is closed Thursdays, except during the summer months. Admission: 18F ($3.60).

The old part of town lies across the river, and it is an easy walk from the ample parking area at the cultural center. Parking is also available in the old town between the church and broad expanse of the **Esplanade du Chapitre**. The view of the Creuse valley is particularly good from the esplanade. **La Maison du Vieux Tapissier** (a display of ancient looms and carpets) is in the old town near the tourist office. Phone: 55-66-32-12.

Hotels

Hôtel de France (6, rue des Déportés—route D942) is a renovated mansion built in 1730, within easy walking distance of the church and esplanade. All rooms have either a bath or shower, and the restaurant is very good. Rates: 300-350F ($60-70). Menus: 70-150F ($14-30). The restaurant is closed Sundays and Mondays during the winter months. Phone: 55-66-10-22.

Just out of town on route N141 toward Clermont-Ferrand is La Seiglière (route de Clermont-Ferrand), which offers all the amenities a traveler could wish for: pool, tennis court, wheelchair access, TV, and a restaurant that serves dinner on a terrace. Closed from December 15 through February 15. Menus: 110-150F ($22-30). Rates: 320F ($64). Phone: 55-66-37-22.

Bourges

Bourges is a city with a population of only about 80,000, small enough to see on foot, yet large enough to provide for days of discovery. The recorded history of Bourges begins with the slaughter of some 40,000 Celts in 52 B.C. by Roman legions securing the area during Caesar's conquest of Gaul. The city assumed the attributes of a massive fortress by the 3rd century, with a stout wall crowned by fifty towers. Today, only remnants of the wall and towers can be found along the perimeter of the Vieille Ville.

Attractions

At the center of town, towering above a roughly cobbled square, is one of the most beautifully inspiring Gothic structures ever built, the Cathédrale St-Étienne. Climbing its North Tower will reward you with a breathtaking view.

After you have seen the cathedral and the Palais Jacques-Coeur, there still remains the Musée du Berry (4, rue des Arènes). Housed in the early 16th-century mansion Hôtel Cujas, a large collection of Celtic and Gallo-Roman artifacts are on display along with many examples of medieval sculpture. Closed Tuesdays and Sundays. Admission: 14F ($2.80). Phone: 48-57-81-15.

The Hôtel Lallemant, halfway between the cathedral and the train station on rue Bourbonneux, is a beautifully preserved (and furnished)

15th- to 16th-century mansion. Admission: 2F ($0.40) and worth every penny. Phone: 48-57-81-17.

For a bit of relief from hobbling over cobblestones, take a few moments to contemplate the formal plantings at the **Jardin des Prés-Fichaux** just north of the train station.

Hotels

Le d'Artagnan (19, place Seraucourt), at the south end of the Vieille Ville, offers all of the modern conveniences. Rates: 265-330F ($53-66). Menus: 65-140F ($13-28). Phone: 48-21-51-51.

Le Christina (5, rue de la Halle) is closer to the cathedral and other points of interest than Le d'Artagnan, but does not have a restaurant. Rooms are comfortable and well furnished. Rates: 210-295F ($42-59). Phone: 48-70-56-50.

Across the Auron River southwest of the old town, but still within walking distance, is the **Hôtel Monitel** (73, rue Barbès). Very up to date and lacking in charm, it still offers good value. La Braisière restaurant is attached. Rates: 230-300F ($46-60). Menus: 75-250F ($15-50). Phone: 48-50-23-62.

Restaurants

Le Jardin Gourmand (15, bis ave. E. Renan) sounds imposing, but the menus are light, and the food is delicious. Menus: 95-230F ($19-46). Phone: 48-21-35-91.

Jacques-Coeur (3, place Jacques-Coeur) is popular and easy to find, so an early call for reservations is a good idea. The food tends toward the more exotic cuts of meat and caloric desserts. After eating here, you'll feel as though you have experienced a real French restaurant. Phone: 48-70-12-72.

For simpler fare, walk to **place Gordaine** at the intersection of rue Bourbonnoux, rue Coursaron, and rue Gambon. There you will find an assortment of cafés and even a hamburger shop.

Chapter 11

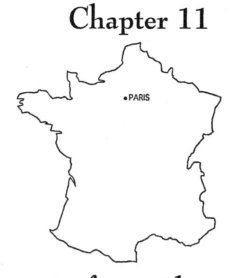

Souvenirs from Abroad: Paris

At ten the next morning, the traffic was heavy on the Périphérique road which circles Paris, but by staying in the second lane, we avoided being forced onto the offramps and, more importantly, avoided vehicles entering the freeway. We swept northward through the Bois de Boulogne and reached the Porte Dauphine, where we left the Périphérique for the slower pace of avenue Foch. It was like coming home when the huge shape of the Arc de Triomphe took form at the end of the broad street.

"Would you like to live here?" Wendy unexpectedly asked.

I surveyed the broad, tree-lined avenue, with its neat rows of townhouses reaching four or five stories up before being capped by verdigris-coated copper roofs. We were traveling through one of the most desirable residential areas in Paris, and I was startled by her question. "We'd need a couple of hundred thousand a year to live in one of those." I gestured broadly at the buildings. "I couldn't even conceive of the idea."

"I don't mean here in Paris! I mean live in France."

"Live in France?" I repeated her question, not sure of the answer she wanted to hear. Best to be honest, I decided. "No. If we lived here, where would we go for vacations?"

"I'm glad you said that." Wendy added, "It's nice to keep some places just for special occasions."

We had reached the Étoile, the star, dominated by the towering Arc de Triomphe, from which all of the grand avenues radiated. I was anxious to return the car, and the wait at the stop light seemed interminable. Finally we were permitted to turn onto the Champs Élysées and see, in the distance, the thin spire of the obelisk brought from Egypt by Napoleon, marking the Place de la Concorde.

"I feel the way the French troops must have felt when they had their victory marches here," Wendy said. "It was such a great trip, that I didn't want it to end, but now . . ." She paused to gather her thoughts. "Now, I just feel triumphant. It's as though we are returning after a great victory. Like Napoleon or de Gaulle."

"Or the Nazis," I added.

She shivered. "Don't remind me."

It took but a few minutes to settle accounts with the car rental agency and to get our luggage to the street level, this time making use of the elevator. A taxi was waiting at the curb, an occurrence that would be expected only in Paris or possibly downtown London, but certainly not in any other city of the world.

Once again settled in at our little hotel just off the rue Royal, we contemplated how the remaining day should be spent. So many possibilities, so little time. I would have been content to take a long nap, but Wendy overrode my lethargy with an enthusiastic plea to visit the modern art exhibits at the Centre Pompidou. She argued that we had bypassed so many museums on our tour that some attention to the finer things of life was long overdue.

It was rather late in the season for frugality, but I had begun to have twinges of anxiety over the spendthrift habits that I had allowed to prevail throughout our trip. "Let's take the Métro instead of a taxi. We'd have to walk only a couple of blocks. Do us good."

Wendy looked at me suspiciously, as though she knew that exercise was not what was on my mind. "We'll get plenty of walking at the museum," she countered, with precise logic.

"We would get there faster on the Métro, and we don't have all that much time left."

"True," she said, "And that would give me time to look in the windows at Hermès again." She knew when she had me.

A booklet of ten tickets, each good for one trip on either bus or underground anywhere within the city, cost thirty-eight francs, about eight dollars. A single taxi ride would cost from thirty to fifty francs, so the savings could be significant, particularly if one were spending several days in Paris. We would use four tickets for the round trip to the museum, and even if we didn't use another one, we would be several dollars ahead.

After a brief stop at Hermès, we checked the map displayed at the Concorde station to find the most direct route to the Pompidou center. Each of the various lines is designated by its ultimate destination, and all stops along the way are clearly marked, making transfers between lines easy. The stations are remarkably clean and well lighted, although some social malcontent had defaced a couple of billboards with spray paint. We boarded a train with the designation "Direction Créteil" which took us to the Châtelet station, only a block from the Pompidou complex.

Once out of the Métro station, we had an uneasy feeling that we were lost, for the Centre Pompidou was nowhere in sight. Wendy tightened her new Hermès scarf about her shoulder as though it were the one thing of certainty in a suddenly confusing world. Actually, it turned out to be an easy matter to locate the Pompidou; all one needed to do was follow the crowd which flowed in a constant stream in one direction. Although we had expected to see the building immediately, it was set back from the street and had been obscured from our view by the intervening office buildings.

The abrupt contrast with the 17th-century architecture of the Beaubourg district was almost shocking. Facing a broad, sloping plaza, the Pompidou thrust its massive girders and looping coils of tubing from the earth itself, as though it were still in the process of a frantic growth which left no time for an exterior skin to form.

The crowd was totally oblivious to the audacity of the building, and we felt conspicuously alone when we stopped to look up. The great mass of people seemed more intent upon enjoying the free entertainment provided by the street musicians, sketch artists, jugglers, and magicians who had taken up station on the plaza in front of the cultural center.

We had just returned from a whirlwind tour of France, experiencing the diversity of the people from north to south and east to west, but here, in the heart of ancient Paris, we found a diversity to equal the biblical Babel. On the corner, an Arabian-looking man bounced an eight-foot-long, sausage-shaped balloon, demonstrating not only the balloon's durability, but his own agility in recovering it from the crowd after a free-flight. Farther down, an Algerian was playing a rippling cadenza on the bottom of a cut-off oil drum. He flashed a dazzling smile and slightly nodded his thanks as a small boy dropped some coins into an open cigar box at his feet, but his hands did not falter as the little hammers extracted music from the steel.

The smell of burning kerosene drifted through the crowd. High upon a raised platform, an emaciated figure dressed in a morning coat somehow managed to keep himself and his costume free of flame as he brought a burning torch to his face. The crowd gasped and tried to back away from the torrent of fire that spewed from the fire-eater's mouth, and then it was over, with only a tenuous thread of smoke to indicate the fire's path. The sound of nervous laughter came from somewhere near the platform, and a small boy clapped his hands and shouted, *"Encore! Encore!"*

The carnival atmosphere made it seem as though the whole of Paris had congregated on the plaza to enjoy the last of the August holiday season at this free show. Old and young alike clustered around the puppet show, watching some variation of Punch and Judy, and the sketch artist was busily turning out rough likenesses in sepia tones for his eager customers. The ice cream vendor was also kept busy scooping up small cones, and I was moving toward him when Wendy reminded me that lunch awaited on the top floor. We passed by the hurdy-gurdy grinder, momentarily amused by the substitution of a cat for the expected monkey, then into the main hall of the Pompidou.

We had not escaped the crowd. The main floor was as packed with people as the baggage claim area at Charles de Gaulle Airport. In the center, a large plastic tube surrounded a moving escalator at least ten feet wide, with each step filled to capacity. It looked like a transparent vacuum cleaner thrust into an ant hill, drawing its occupants upward into the unknown. We were in no hurry to join that throng on the escalator, and so we wandered about the main floor and looked at an exhibit of impressionist paintings, deciding that most of them seemed second-rate when compared to those we had seen at the Musée d'Orsay.

We finally admitted that, if we were to see any of the major exhibits, we would have to brave the escalator, despite the fact that the mass of people there never seemed to thin. The moving steps were so wide that six to ten people could be accommodated on each, the exact figure being determined by the number of backpacks and small children, not to mention the girth of each passenger. The second floor was of little interest to us, being given over to the art of home furnishing; nor did it seem to interest anyone else, and the escalator to the third floor remained crowded. Halfway up it shuddered to a stop, and Wendy made an impossible attempt to grasp a handrail. Not sure of whether to be disgusted or amused, we stuck out the rest of the ride and finally made our way to the top floor.

Once we were in view of the top, we saw the reason for the long delays; although there were three ticket booths, there was but a single ticket seller. With numerous discounts available for every category from child to student to senior citizen to wounded veteran, it took an inordinate amount of time to check the documents required before a ticket could be dispensed. Two girls in front of us had to rummage through their knapsacks to produce the proper student passes. When it came our turn, I bought two regular-priced tickets, feeling that the discount available to us as seniors was not worth the time involved, particularly for those hundreds of people waiting on the steps below.

We discovered that the exhibits on the top floor are not permanent and are changed every two weeks, so one can only be certain of expecting the unexpected. It was a happy moment to be free of the crowd, and it made little difference what we would see. As we wandered into the almost empty halls, the idea formed that perhaps the clever French had designed all of the strictures on the escalators precisely to limit the number of people entering the exhibits.

Wendy was delighted to discover rooms filled with fauvist paintings. Most of the names were obviously German, like Kichner and Beckmann, although I did recognize the French artists Georges Rouault and Maurice de Vlaminck. The canvases were covered with bold forms in intense colors, revolutionary in their simple, vigorous drama. Still, it seemed to me that if a sampling of the exhibit had been displayed on a lower floor, the escalator subterfuge would have been totally unnecessary.

Nearby we found a room devoted to Edouard Vuillard, a painter who was obviously influenced by Matisse, but who handled the brush with love rather than the apparent anger displayed in the other rooms. Lush interiors opened upon sunlit gardens and countryside vistas, creating a world of comfort and gentle delight. Once again, Wendy and I were in agreement that this one room more than compensated for the tribulations suffered on the escalator.

After lunch, we were reminded that one of nature's immutable laws seems to be that what goes up slowly comes down quickly, and within minutes we had descended to the still-crowded plaza. The hot afternoon sun was beating down ferociously, and although the fire-eater had apparently retired for the day, the balloon bouncers were still slamming their gigantic toys against the pavement to send them vaulting into the air. Wendy left my side for a moment to contribute a few coins for the cat which was pretending to be an organ-grinder's monkey. *"Pour le chat,"* she said and then explained to me, "I wanted him to know that it was for the cat."

"He'll use it to feed himself first."

"Probably, but at least he'll think of the cat."

"Of course he will."

"I've had enough of crowds," I said. "Let's walk to the Luxembourg Gardens. It should be nice and cool there, with a place to sit down."

"How far is it?"

"Shouldn't be more than a few blocks." I was not really sure of the distance, but it had looked fairly close on the map at the Métro station. "Besides, we could make reservations for dinner at that bistro where they play jazz."

Wendy somewhat reluctantly agreed, and we set out. We walked six blocks down the rue du Renard, across the bridge to the boulevard du Palais de Justice, which in turn led across the Ile de la Cité to another bridge connecting us to the Left Bank. The broad boulevard Saint-Michel stretched ahead into the distance. "Only a few blocks more," I said, trying to be reassuring.

Wendy looked at me glumly, but plodded along at a steady pace until we crossed the boulevard Saint-Germain, the main thoroughfare of the Latin Quarter. "Okay, how much farther?"

"I'm sure we're on the right street. It can't be more than a few blocks now." An empty taxi whizzed by, and I saw her look longingly after it.

"Well, if we get there, I'm not walking another step. I'm just going to sit in the park until you find a taxi to take us back to the hotel. The tone of her voice let me know that this was a point to be conceded without argument.

Three blocks farther along and I was about to join the forces of rebellion. I was furtively checking each corner for a taxi when the wrought-iron fence surrounding the gardens appeared. "See," I said, not trying to disguise the note of triumph. "And there's the Luxembourg Métro." I pointed up the street at the small circular sign above a narrow stairway.

A moment later, Wendy was relaxing on a shaded bench, enjoying the views of flowers and formal hedges, while I was making dinner reservations across the street at the bistro, Le Petit Journal. "The Little Newspaper" seemed a peculiar name for a place specializing in jazz, but the Left Bank was notorious for adopting strange names for its cafés, such as the famous Les

Deux Magots, an unappetizing name that begs translation. Once we were assured of dinner at eight and good seats for the show, I hurried back to Wendy. She was ready for a leisurely stroll through the gardens, but to my relief, still insisted upon taking a taxi back to the hotel.

In the early evening, we set out for our last night in Paris. We descended the stairs into the Métro station Madeleine and stopped in front of the map to determine the most direct course to the Luxembourg station. "We are here," I said as I put a finger on the spot. "We take the train in the direction of Mairie d'Issy, get off at Montparnasse, transfer to the Porte d'Orléans line, get off at Denfert-Rocherean and catch the Luxembourg line to our destination."

"Sounds easy, when you put it like that," Wendy said.

"Maybe I missed something," I replied as I checked the map again. I was appalled at the number of transfers, and I realized that we would have to travel on secondary lines, which meant long waits between trains. "Ahhhh," I said in my most judicious tone, "there is a quicker way. Don't say anything, just come along." I took her by the hand and led her back up the stairs, out of the station. At the top, I dropped the packet of remaining Métro tickets onto the lap of a panhandler, and we made our way to the taxi stand.

The following morning found us on the jet, with seat backs in the upright position and seat belts fastened, as though to prevent our changing our minds and escaping back to Paris. The plane moved slowly to its place, sending up waves of vapor from the thin sheets of water remaining from the night's shower on the runway. Wendy broke our silence by asking if I was sorry that we were leaving.

"Just thinking of the things we missed," I answered.

"Like seeing the *aurochs* in the Dordogne?"

The plane began picking up speed. "No—more like sitting on the steps of Sacré-Coeur and being surprised by the sunset. Just the two of us, quietly watching the lights of Paris slowly flicker on."

She squeezed my hand and murmured, "Maybe next time," as the plane leaped upward off the runway.

A slow turn, while the plane gained altitude, allowed us a last view of the rooftops of suburban Paris, then we arced above the clouds into the dazzling morning sky, and France was gone.

~ On Your Own ~

Souvenir Shopping

The diversity of France is nowhere more evident than in its capital, Paris. Here, if you know where to look, you can find everything from haute couture (on avenue Victor-Hugo or rue du Faubourg-St.-Honoré) to worn-out hand-me-downs at the marchés aux puces (flea markets).

Although a smart shop with exactly what you want may mysteriously appear in the most unlikely neighborhood, in general, Paris may be separated into three specialty regions. On the **Right Bank**, from the Opéra and place Vendôme to the avenue Montaigne, you will find the "name" shops dealing in luxury items. Trendy, *au courant* shops dominate the redeveloped **Les Halles**, the **Marais**, and the **Bastille** areas. The Left Bank region around **St.-Germain-des-Prés** offers fashionable shops for the bargain-hunting student, as well as shops that sell touristy T-shirts.

Most of the **flea markets** are open only on weekends, with Mondays reserved for clearance sales. Of course, the best stuff is sold on Saturday mornings. The largest and best known is **St.-Ouen** at avenue de la Porte de Clingnancourt, with nearly 3,000 stalls in a half-mile area. Take bus #56 or the Métro to Porte de Clingnancourt.

If you are particularly interested in clothing, the flea market at **Porte de Montreuil** may be more to your liking. For bric-a-brac, the flea market at **Port de Vanves** offers the best bargains. Plan on a full day at any of these (the Métro ride can take an hour) and wear comfortable shoes. Credit cards will not work at these markets, so carry francs in small-denomination bills and coins. It is hard to plead poverty if all you can produce is a 500-franc note.

If the hassle of a flea market is not your style, but you still want bargains, try visiting one of the *dépôts-vents* (**resale shops**) where you can buy slightly-used or sometimes new (samples or discontinued lines) merchandise with famous labels. Both **Caméléon** and **Ellipse** can be reached from the Métro Station Victor-Hugo. Take the Métro to Pompe to visit the largest of these shops, **Réciproque**. If you take a taxi, the addresses are: Caméléon, 13, rue Gustave-Courbet; Ellipse, 26, rue Gustave-Courbet; and Réciproque, 95, rue de la Pompe.

Everyone is familiar with the book stalls along the Seine quays near the cathedral, but there are many other specialty markets. For stamps, the **Marché aux Timbres** at the intersection of avenues Marigny and Gabriel can be reached from Métro station Champs-Élysées-Clemenceau. The stalls are open Thursdays, Saturdays, Sundays, and holidays.

Although purchases from this market cannot be brought to the United States, a visit to the flower market at **place Louis-Lépine**, on the Ile de la Cité, is a refreshing experience. On Sundays, the Marché aux Fleurs is expanded to include the **Marché aux Oiseaux**, a bird market of depressingly large proportions.

Although it seems that every museum has a **gift shop**, the one at the **Centre Georges Pompidou**, which occupies most of the main floor, is by far the best. Here you will find books, posters, cards, and slides covering all areas of France—a veritable wonderland for souvenirs.

Pot-Pourri

ATMs: Automatic teller machines are located at banks in all of the major cities in Europe. You receive the inter-bank rate, the most advantageous exchange rate, when you withdraw cash. However, if you use a credit card, interest is charged from the day you receive the cash. If you plan to use automatic teller machines to obtain local currency, check with the bank that issued your card before leaving home to be certain that your PIN number will work overseas.

Auberge: A country inn where you can expect a good meal of simple country food. If you take a room, you will be expected to also take dinner.

Auberge de Jeunesse: A youth hostel; signs will often show the letters "AJ."

Automobile Rentals: Available rental cars come in all sizes and degrees of luxury. The basic car is small, with a four-cylinder engine, stick shift, and no air conditioning. This will cost from $30 to $35 per day, complete with all insurance and unlimited mileage. You will find the basic car to be ideal for poking around country lanes and back roads in ancient villages, most of which were laid out long before automobiles were invented. If you want something beyond the basics, plan on paying $5 to $10 extra per day for each feature desired. Cars with automatic shifts are fairly common, and this feature will cost less than will air conditioning.

Autoroute: The major highways and freeways of France all carry numbers. If the number is preceded by an "N" it is a national *autoroute*, parts of which may be subject to tolls. When you see a blue sign with the word *péage*, you know that you will have to pay, sometimes dearly.

Bistro: An intimate combination of bar and café with a limited menu, generally of simple food, and casual entertainment.

Brasserie: A short-order restaurant, usually owned by a brewery.

Centre Ville: The town center, where you will usually find the tourist office, as well as the main church or cathedral, the town hall, police station, post office, etc. Here you will generally find specialty stores, not supermarkets.

Cheese: The French take cheese seriously, with over four hundred varieties officially recognized by the government and awarded the designation "Appellation d'Origine," and the list is still growing. Although other countries may challenge France with individual cheeses, no other country can lay claim to such a variety. Cheese is a standard course on most menus, and it's sometimes the high point of a meal.

Clothing: But for the height of summer and the depth of winter, temperatures are moderate in France, quite similar to those of the West Coast of the United States. For women, pants and skirts, with an assortment of tops, will do nicely for everyday wear, but one dressy dress is recommended for special occasions. For men, a couple of pairs of washable slacks and an all-purpose, lightweight jacket will see you through. A shirt and tie take little room and will be expected at fancier establishments. A good pair of lightweight walking shoes is a must. For men, there are several brands of shoes which can take a shine and double as dress shoes. Women will have to take along an extra pair of shoes for dress occasions.

Credit Cards: Cash is still king for roadside purchases, flea markets and produce markets; however, in this age of plastic, we have long since discarded carrying large sums of cash or even travelers' checks. We have found that either a Mastercard or Visa will be acceptable at almost any hotel, restaurant, or gas station. The American Express card is generally accepted at the more posh resort hotels and restaurants, but even in these places, you will often be asked to use one of the other cards. In an emergency, though, you may find the American Express card to be invaluable, since it has no credit limit.

Currency: It is a good idea to arrive with some local currency, which you should purchase from a bank or exchange window at the airport before leaving the United States. It is always advisable to have some local currency and coins at hand for taxis, parking, snacks, and other incidentals. Although U.S. dollars are universally accepted, you will not get a very good exchange rate from a taxi driver. Once in France, the best exchange rates are through the ATMs.

Drink: Wine is presumed to be the national beverage of France, but beer is consumed in greater quantities. You will find that most of the sidewalk cafés are owned by breweries. If you crave water with your meals, order a bottle of either plain (*natural*) or carbonated (*gas*). If you desire stronger stuff, expect to pay dearly because of taxes. Do not expect wines from a famous château to be inexpensive; the prices are not much lower than in the United States. However, if you have an adventurous spirit, try some of the lesser-known labels. You will be pleasantly surprised.

Driving: If traffic-jammed cities are avoided, driving is a pleasure in France. The road system is extensive and well maintained, with even the gravel roads in the rural areas regularly graded. Farm animals, tractors, and bicyclists are the chief road hazards you are likely to encounter.

The "rule of the right," which states that the vehicle on the right has the right of way, is often superseded by signs reading "Cédez le Passage," the equivalent of the American "Yield." Stop signs leave no doubt, as they are identical to the signs at home. Traffic lights are placed well back from intersections and are out of the line of sight of the driver; however, they are duplicated in miniature at eye level on the light standards, so as to be easily visible.

A valid driver's license (your U.S. license is okay) and proof of insurance should be with you in the car whenever you drive.

Seat belts are mandatory, and you will be stopped and fined by the police if you have not buckled up. Children under the age of ten are not permitted to ride in the front seat or to stand when the vehicle is in motion.

Should you be stopped for a driving violation, expect to be fined on the spot, with no judicial hearing or right of appeal. Fines will range from 1,300 francs ($250) for speeding to 5,000 francs ($1,000) for drunk driving. These must be paid in cash—credit cards and travelers' checks will not work here! Speed limits are clearly posted, although they are often ignored by the French drivers. If you choose to follow their lead, be sure you have sufficient cash on hand to cover your bet.

Electricity: Electric current is a standard 220 volt, 50 cycles. Do not try your hair dryer or electric shaver without an adapter. To conserve energy, French hotels are often equipped with timers that turn off the hall lights after a very short time. It doesn't pay to dawdle, but should you be left in the dark, a touch on the red-glowing switch will turn on the lights.

Food: Good food is one of the glories of France, and dinner is usually the big meal. A full dinner is an occasion and you should plan on it lasting several hours. Expect to pay $100 to $150 per person to dine at a three-star restaurant, but in the country, you will often find an equally delightful experience for from $25 to $50. Breakfast (*le petit déjeuner*) is usually included in your room rate or is available at nominal cost. A very light affair, it consists of coffee, tea, or hot chocolate and a roll. Supplements are usually available at additional cost—a glass of orange juice may double the price. Settle for the meager breakfast and reward yourself with a mid-morning snack at a *salon de thé* or a sidewalk café.

Gasoline: Gasoline is *essence* in French and diesel fuel is *gasoil*. All rental cars will use unleaded *essence* and do quite well on the lowest grade. Both Visa and Mastercard are readily accepted at most stations, but your gasoline credit card from the U.S. will be refused, even if the station boasts the same name.

Guidebooks: The *Michelin* guides reign supreme for comprehensive travel information about France; after all, France is home to Michelin. The basic red guide covers food and lodging, and the regional green guides cover everything else, from history and architecture to local customs and festivals. Unfortunately, many of the green guides are not available in English translation. Other guidebooks that have proved helpful over the years are *Fodor's*, *Frommer's*, and the *Penguin Guide to France*. For a more personalized approach, *France a la Carte* by Richard Binns is worth a look. If you are into gastronomy, *Gault Millau* will provide you with a list of the best restaurants to be found in any sizable French town. For those with a more restricted cash flow, *The Rough Guide to France* is both accurate and up to date with the latest in economy travel.

Health: If you have problems that require specific medication, be sure to bring along a written prescription from your doctor, just in case your supply is lost or becomes contaminated. In emergencies, you will be surprised at the speed and competence with which you will be attended. In France, doctors will even make house calls at night, and hospitals do not require the lengthy forms and guarantees of payment so common in the U.S.

Holidays: Holidays are a serious matter to the traveler, because most businesses, including banks, will be closed. Restaurants generally do not close, but will usually be filled early. Major national holidays:

January 1—New Years' Day

Easter Sunday and Monday

Forty days after Easter—Ascension Day

Seventh Sunday and Monday after Easter—Pentecost

May 1—May Day/Labor Day

May 8—V-Day

July 14—Bastille Day

August 15—Assumption of the Virgin

November 1—All Saints' Day

November 11—Armistice Day

December 25—Christmas Day

Hôtels: The name is generally used, as would be expected, to indicate a place where travelers may rent a room, but it's also used to indicate a fancy private townhouse or mansion. Do not seek a room at the Hôtel de Ville, the town hall.

Insurance: France has a national, universal health plan, and doctors and hospitals are willing to take care of any tourist in need of health service. Payment is expected, but most health plans in the U.S. will cover the costs if you have arranged in advance for the proper documentation to carry with you. Auto insurance is a must, and proof of coverage is demanded if you are involved in an accident. Many credit cards offer such coverage when they are used to rent a car, but it is wise to understand the process involved in making a claim before you leave the U.S. I think of insurance as a way to reduce hassles—the extra charge for complete coverage by the car rental company amounts to the price of a couple of beers per day, and I think it well worth the money. However, for luxury cars with air conditioning, the costs will be extremely high, and probably not to your advantage.

Language: French will always remain a foreign language to anyone not born and raised in France. However, considering that four years of

English study are required of all French students, communication is generally possible, even though occasionally awkward. Don't be discouraged by your Parisian waiter; finding one who will admit to understanding an American speaking French may be impossible, but you will discover that the understanding of your speech will seem to increase relative to your distance from Paris.

Laundry: Hotels discourage washing of clothes in the room, but if you are judicious, a few pieces of underwear and socks hanging in the room, but not in the window or on the balcony, will be overlooked. For heavier loads, look for a laundromat, a *laverie automatique*, and have plenty of one-franc coins on hand. Dry-cleaning shops are expensive by U.S. standards, but if you need one, look for the sign "Pressé."

Lodgings: *Chambres d'hôte* are bed-and-breakfast guest houses; some offer a private bath, but most often these facilities are shared with others.

A *tables d'hôte* will provide you with a good home-cooked dinner as well as a chance to become acquainted with your host and family over the dinner table. A stay at a *tables d'hôte* presupposes a working knowledge of the French language. Seldom listed in guidebooks, their locations may be obtained from the regional tourist bureau.

Hostelries provide rudimentary lodgings along with a basic breakfast; shared bathroom facilities are to be expected.

An *auberge* will place the major emphasis on food, with the sleeping accommodations taking a secondary role. If you take a room at an *auberge*, you will be expected to have dinner there.

Facilities listed as "Logis de France" include everything from converted castles to rustic hunting lodges. These are generally luxurious accommodations and are priced accordingly.

Hôtels may be with or without restaurants. They are regularly inspected and rated by the government, with the rating on display at the *hôtel* entrance in the form of a sign bearing from one to three white stars on a blue background. Although the stars are supposedly given to indicate the various levels of comfort to be expected, one can draw a direct correlation between the number of stars and the number of rooms with private bath facilities.

Luggage: Assume that you will be carrying everything up several flights of stairs each day. Pack light to save your strength for more pleasurable activities. A small carry-on bag should contain the essentials for a couple of days' living, just in case your check-through bags are lost or misdirected by the airline. Avoid luggage that proclaims, "Here is a wealthy person." Old Gray looks so disreputable that no one would think of breaking into a car to steal it. Finally, when in public places, particularly airports or railway stations, keep your bags with you. Terrorists have been known to abandon explosive luggage, and any baggage without an attendant is suspect and may be seized by station police.

Métro: The subway system of Paris is a very efficient (usually) and inexpensive way to get around the city. Tickets and passes are purchased at any of the stations. Once you have entered through a ticket-taking turnstile, you may transfer to any connecting line, as long as you do not go through an exit turnstile. The same tickets and passes may be used on the buses. Easy-to-read maps of the system are posted at every station, and all of the cars carry a schematic outline of the particular route you are on, so it is easy to tell which station is coming next.

Passports: Keep your own passport with you, not with someone else in your party, and most definitely not in a suitcase in your hotel. A young American woman told us the following story of her experience with passports while she was studying in Paris:

"Five of us from school decided to check out some of the nightlife, so we dressed up in our best jeans—you know, the ones that are so tight you can't put anything in the pockets. Anyway, I was the only one carrying a purse, so all the girls gave me their passports to carry. We went to this little café with really loud music, and while I was sitting at the bar, this little weasel comes up behind me and tries to get his hand in my rear pocket. I turned around real fast and swung my purse at him. It caught him right on the face, and he fell over backwards. The purse came open and all of the passports flew out. The little weasel was on the floor with a bloody face, covered with passports and screaming bloody murder. Someone, probably the bartender, called the police, and the next thing I know, I'm being held as a possible terrorist—why else would anyone be carrying so many passports? They put me in a police van and took me to the headquarters, asking me all sorts of crazy questions. Finally my friends showed up—they'd had to find a taxi—and the police matched their faces with the passports. They let me go with a warning not to carry anyone else's passport. It's only funny now, when I think back on it."

Picnics: A loaf of bread, a jug of wine, add a bit of cheese and some fresh fruit for a dining experience that is refreshing and cheap.

Everything you need can be purchased at a supermarket: a sharp knife, a corkscrew, paper plates, a roll of paper towels (also handy for cleaning the windshield), and don't forget the plastic cups. Of course, they also sell food, but it is much more enjoyable if you shop the little stores and bakeries along your way.

Police: Other than asking for directions, we have never had any contact with the French police; nonetheless, it is good to have some knowledge of their function and authority. There are two separate divisions, the Police National and the Gendarmerie, but for the tourist, there is little distinction between the two. Generally, it is the Gendarmerie that is used for the heavy duty stuff like our SWAT teams, while the Police National investigates crimes and metes out traffic fines. However, both will respond to calls for help and either can make arrests or levy fines.

Restaurants: This is where you go for the full treatment. Unlike cafés, *brasseries*, and *bistros*, restaurants are likely to be formal in decor and clientele. Neckties and jackets are expected to be worn by men and dressy apparel by women. Plan for the evening's entertainment to consist of eating.

Rez de Chaussée: This is the ground floor of any building (the elevator button will indicate "RC"). The first floor in France is equivalent to the second floor in the U.S. The RC button is clearly marked in most elevators.

Shopping: It is advisable to use credit cards when paying for any large-ticket purchases, particularly if you are having the shop pack and ship to your home. Use of the card will make any adjustments easy in the event that your purchase arrives damaged or, worse, does not arrive at all. A complaint to the credit card company will result in a charge back to the store and a credit to your account. Just be sure that you save all of your duplicate charge slips. Sales slips are also handy to have on hand when you make out your Customs declaration upon returning to the U.S. Note: Be extremely cautious about purchasing items made of animal materials, especially ivory or reptile skin; U.S. Customs may confiscate any items made from an endangered species. Wendy had to surrender the tortoise-shell comb that I had so laboriously purchased without giving a thought to its origins.

Syndicat d'Initiative: The office of tourist information, sometimes listed as "Maison du Tourisme." Your best friends in France are here. They can tell you what is most interesting to see in the area, as well as where hotel rooms are available. Sometimes they will even make telephone calls to reserve rooms for you.

Taxis: Cabs are plentiful and relatively inexpensive in Paris, but they are few and relatively expensive in the smaller cities. It is usually better to take a hotel within walking distance of the things you wish to see, than to depend upon taxis. Of course, there will be times when fatigue sets in and a taxi is the quickest and most energy-conserving way to get off your feet and back to your hotel.

Telephones: You will find the cost of telephone service from your hotel to be exorbitant, but if you are making only one or two calls, it is probably worth the expense. The pay phones in France are switching to the use of cards rather than coins (Paris is almost completely converted), and without a card it is impossible to place a call. Cards, which work like bus passes, are for a specific number of telephone units and may be purchased at post offices and some tobacco shops. The international country code for France is 33, and the area codes are represented by the first two digits of the number.

Time: France is one hour east of Greenwich Mean Time, which puts it six hours earlier than New York and nine hours earlier than San Francisco.

Tipping: In most restaurants, your tip is included with the check, indicated by the words "Service Compris." It is always a good idea to have a few one- and five-franc coins handy for baggage handlers, chambermaids and taxi drivers. In general, do as you would at home: 10% to the taxi driver and hair dresser; two francs per bag to the bell boy; five francs per person per night to the chambermaid will keep everyone happy.

Toiletries: Even the cheapest hotel will usually provide soap and towels if you have rented a room with bath or shower. Sometimes you will find shampoo and even bath lotion included, but what you will seldom find is a wash cloth. Better bring your own.

Toilets: For the most part, the old open-air street toilets have been replaced with modern coin-operated, self-sanitizing chambers in the major cities. However, the old adage "Carry a roll of paper," still applies in the more rural parts of the country, and many of the older cafés and *bistros* which are equipped with the infamous "Turkish" toilets.

Tourist Offices: Even the smaller towns will have a designated office. Follow the signs to the Syndicat d'Initiative.

Travel Agents: Since Murphy's Law applies particularly to the traveler, the use of a travel agent to arrange all of the particulars of a trip has the added advantage of providing a convenient whipping boy to blame for any unexpected inconveniences. However, tickets issued by the airline will generally be accepted by other airlines, but airline tickets issued by a travel agent are often not accepted by airlines other than the one designated on the ticket. This may require you to purchase an additional ticket if for some unforeseen reason an alternate airline must be used. This is another good reason to carry a credit card.

Travelers' Checks: Travelers' checks have largely been replaced by the more convenient credit card. Although they are accepted by most businesses, you will often be charged a service fee. This is most onerous at hotels, where you may be charged as much as 10%. If the feeling of security engendered by the promise of replacement if the checks are lost or stolen is more important than efficiency and economy, then bring them along. Exchange travelers' checks for the local currency at banks to avoid service fees. Be sure to have your passport with you when doing so.

Value Added Tax: If you are doing any extensive buying, you should know that a tax of up to 30% is included in the price of everything. A refund of this tax (the VAT) is available to foreign tourists who stay less than six months and make a minimum of 2000F ($400) of purchases at any given store. Some stores will even process the paperwork involved in a refund for you, but you should enquire as to whether this service is available before you buy. If you must handle the refund yourself, the store will provide you with the papers (and return envelope) that you will need to turn in to the French Customs office at the air-port when you depart.

Water: Tap water is generally as safe to drink throughout Western Europe as it is in the U.S. Most problems encountered by travelers are the result of a different mineral content rather than any contamination. If you order bottled water at a restaurant, specify the brand name or you may be served tap water in a bottle. Should you suffer from a mild diarrhea in the first few days after arrival, it is best that you drink more water to avoid dehydration and to flush out the system. Only if the symptoms persist beyond one or two days should you resort to the use of medication.

Weather: In the summer, rain can happen, so an umbrella and light-weight plastic raincoat can make the difference between sitting in a hotel lobby or enjoying your trip. In the winter, if you are like me, you will stay off the country roads and enjoy the life of the big cities—indoors. Finally, to convert from Celsius to Fahrenheit, multiply Celsius degrees by 1.8 and add 32. If that is too much trouble, just remember that your normal body temperature is about 37 degrees Celsius and gauge the weather accordingly.

Index